Jesus's Manifesto

Jesus's Manifesto

The Sermon on the Plain

ROMAN A. MONTERO

Foreword by James Crossley

RESOURCE *Publications* · Eugene, Oregon

JESUS'S MANIFESTO
The Sermon on the Plain

Resource Publications
An Imprint of Wipf and Stock Publishers
199 W. 8th Ave., Suite 3
Eugene, OR 97401

www.wipfandstock.com

PAPERBACK ISBN: 978-1-5326-7603-1
HARDCOVER ISBN: 978-1-5326-7604-8
EBOOK ISBN: 978-1-5326-7605-5

Manufactured in the U.S.A.   MARCH 29, 2019

Contents

Foreword

CRITICAL SCHOLARSHIP HAS LONG had a history of materialist readings of Christian origins. In the nineteenth century and early twentieth century some of the biggest names from across the Left (e.g. Engels, Proudhon, Kautsky) produced analyses based on class and power. These were works that took critical biblical scholarship seriously and were, for a while, taken seriously by critical biblical scholarship. After the First World War, the Russian Revolution and the rise of the Soviet Union, this academic past was forgotten or dismissed in mainstream scholarship of Christian origins, even if such scholarship continued outside. However, the social and ideological upheavals of the 1960s led to the re-emergence of such scholarship in the mainstream over the next few decades. In terms of the historical Jesus, the work of Richard Horsley was among the most prominent. Such scholarship took new directions, by bringing gender-critical questions in to discussion with materialist ones, as in the work of Elisabeth Schüssler Fiorenza and Halvor Moxnes, for instance.

There have been ebbs and flows of such scholarship and, after a period where conservative and liberal scholarship has dominated, there has been a revival of questions relating to class in recent years. Jesus's Manifesto belongs to this revitalized materialist tendency in contemporary critical scholarship of Christian origins and is an important contribution. Roman Montero takes seriously the idea of class as a concept for understanding early Christian texts and in this case the presentation of Jesus's teaching in Luke's Sermon on the Plain. Moreover, this is not a romanticized or naïve reading of class and conflict as Montero, in the best materialist traditions, rightly reveals the complexities of socioeconomic interests in Galilee at the time of Jesus. Anyone with critical inclinations and who wants a fuller explanation of Christian origins needs to understand what Montero is doing in this book and take seriously ideas of class, economics, and historical change—irrespective of their perspective.

But this is also a book that will interest critical exegetes. There is a great deal of (convincing and sensible) close reading of the text and how the text is bound up with socioeconomic issues. Montero reveals a knowledge of a breadth of primary sources from a range of Greco-Roman contexts, including Jewish texts. What is important about understanding such texts is how they can be reapplied in different context and how their more radical potential can be realized in contexts removed from aristocratic interests— something that would happen long after the texts were written and right up to the present. Montero's discussion of these texts should prove illuminating to anyone who engages with the Sermon on the Plain, or indeed any of the related texts in the Gospel tradition which deal with unequal economic distribution.

Montero is not content settling with reading the Sermon on the Plain as simply a collection of ethical injunctions. Building on his previous work, he (rightly in my view) locates the importance of community formation and contextualizes this in terms of 'communism' which is understood in an anthropological sense of social relations, rather than a more anachronistic reading in the modern political sense, though the two, of course, could potentially be connected. This, in my opinion, is a significant contribution to critical scholarship on the historical Jesus (and indeed Acts and Christian origins) which advances the discussion of how we understand community formation. Again, whatever the perspective, scholars should be engaging with this argument in detail.

I was especially interested to see that a comparison was made between Jesus and the radical English priest John Ball who died in 1381 during what is customarily called the Peasants' Revolt. The comparison between the two deserves further research, such as in terms of eschatology and their dramatic challenges to wealth and power. Montero's claims about the respective textual representations of Jesus and Ball is also an intriguing addition to a comparative study. But what the comparison with Ball also does is to remind us that challenges to injustice and visions of a better world have never been entirely suppressed and, even in contexts of failure and loss, no matter how unlikely the situation may seem to be, they can—and no doubt will—re-emerge.

Montero's discussion of community formation is crucial if we want to think about not only how such ideas have thrived and can thrive but how they can be implemented. Academics proclaiming that they are progressive, liberal, 'a bit left wing', and so on is not good enough by itself. To reword an older saying, the last thing liberal academics want is anything too revolutionary that will threaten their position of privileged complaining about the status quo. A little exaggerated, perhaps, but if academics are to be genuinely concerned with the material interests of the working class, then getting involved with the material interests of the working class is vital otherwise we can only realistically categorize such academics as 'liberal'. And to sustain any potential movement with working class interests in mind, then such serious thinking about community formation, community integration, and organization of a disciplined alternative is absolutely necessary to keep firm against the inevitable and sustained attacks.

JAMES CROSSLEY
Professor of Bible, Society, and Politics
St Mary's University

I

Jesus's Manifesto

ACCORDING TO THE MERRIAM Webster dictionary, "manifesto" is defined as "a written statement declaring publicly the intentions, motives, or views of its issuer." Among the most famous manifestos in history are the Declaration of Independence of the United States, the Declaration of the Rights of Man and Citizen, and the Communist Manifesto. These manifestos have changed the course of human history and have in many ways created the modern world. The Sermon on the Plain has often been thought of as an ethical text, or an ethical sermon, and it certainly is that; however, I claim that it is more than that—it is a manifesto. I claim that the Sermon on the Plain is far more important, profound, and morally pressing, than all the fore-mentioned manifestos put together.

Much of one's interpretation of, and classification of, the Sermon on the Plain will depend on how one interprets both the goal of the writer of the Gospel of Luke (or his sources), as well as the ministry of the historical Jesus. My position is that the message of the Sermon on the Plain largely goes back to the historical Jesus—and that it is a manifesto for an eschato-logical community: a community dedicated to serving God in light of and in support of God's eschatological plan. My position is that the historical context of the Sermon is that of early first-century Jewish polemics about the interpretation of Torah regulations and scripture; as well as a Jewish apocalyptic worldview, and a Galilean population under domination by Rome and exploitation by the local elites. I claim that the Sermon on the Plain lays out an eschatological vision: a vision of what God is doing and what he will do in the future—followed by a declaration of what must be done in light of that vision and in support of it. It is in this way that I say that the Sermon on the Plain is Jesus's manifesto.

Although much work has been done in redaction criticism, in breaking down the words of Jesus as recorded in the gospels to find layers of redaction and the use of various sources; overall, much of what is recorded in the Sermon on the Plain—at least the vision and ideas within the Sermon—can be attributed to the historical Jesus. I do not mean here to enter into the exhaustive (and exhausting) debate over sources and criteria of authenticity; my argument takes a different tack. The task I have given myself here is to make sense of the Sermon and see if it can be made sense of as a reflection of Jesus's teachings within his context. A good model for thinking of the Sermon on the Plain's relationship to the actual words of Jesus, I propose, is the way the sermons of the 14th-century peasant revolutionary and Lollard priest John Ball were presented in the account of a contemporary, Jean Froissart, in his *Chronicles of England, France, Spain, and other places adjoining.* In that work Jean says the following about John Ball:

> A crazy priest in the county of Kent, called John Ball, who, for his absurd preaching, had been thrice confined in the prison of the archbishop of Canterbury, was greatly instrumental in inflaming them with those ideas. He was accustomed, every Sunday after mass, as the people were coming out of the church, to preach to them in the market place and assemble a crowd around him; to whom he would say,—
>
> "My good friends, things cannot go on in England, nor ever will until everything shall be in common; when there shall neither be vassal nor lord, and all distinctions levelled; when the lords shall be no more masters than ourselves. How ill have they used us! And for what reason to they thus hold us in bondage? Are we not all descended from the same parents, Adam and Eve? And what can they show, or what reasons give, why they should be more the masters than ourselves? Except, perhaps, in making us labour and work, for them to spend. They are clothed in velvets and rich stuffs, ornamented with ermine and other furs, while we are forced to wear poor cloth. They have wines, spices, and fine bread, when we have only rye and the refuse of the straw; and, if we drink, it must be water. They have handsome seats and manors, when we must brave the wind and rain in our labours in the field; but it is from our labour they have wherewith to support their pomp. We are called slaves; and if we do not perform our services, we are beaten, and we have not any sovereign to whom we can complain, or who wishes to hear us and do us justice. Let us go to the king,

who is young, and remonstrate with him on our servitude, telling him we must have it otherwise, or that we shall find a remedy for it ourselves. If we wait on him in a body, all those who come under the appellation of slaves, or are held in bondage, will follow us, in the hopes of being free. When the king shall see us, we shall obtain a favourable answer, or we must then seek ourselves to amend our condition."

With such words as these did John Ball harangue the people at his village every Sunday after mass, for which he was much beloved by them. (Froissart, *Chronicles of England, France, Spain, and the Adjoining Countries,* 652–653 [Johnes])

To be clear, the actual content of the sermon is not the important part for the model I am presenting. I included the whole sermon mainly because I find it to be an engaging and exciting sermon. What is important is the way Jean Froissart presents the sermon: This is what John Ball was accustomed to preach: "with such words." So although Jean Froissart records a very detailed script that holds together and makes a coherent argument, he is not recording any one particular speech of John Ball; nor is he collecting quotes from various speeches and stringing them together in a kind of anthology. Instead, Jean Froissart is writing out a kind of prototype sermon, the "kind" of sermon that John Ball would give. Jean Froissart is basically saying that had you listened to any specific sermon of John Ball, it would sound very much like, and be making the same point as, the prototype sermon he is presenting.

This is more or less the model we should use when comparing the Sermon on the Plain to the actual historical teachings of Jesus. What is recorded for us in Luke 6:20–49 is not likely a word-for-word speech given by Jesus, or a translation of a word-for-word speech; nor is it a collection of Jesus's sayings; nor is it an ideological representation of some teachings of the historical Jesus, which is ultimately mostly Luke's (or Q's) invention in the form we have it. It is, rather, more likely a literary prototype of the kind of speech that Jesus made (perhaps put in the context of an actual historical speech that Jesus gave), and a representation of Jesus's teachings that is reasonably faithful to the teachings and speeches of the historical Jesus.[1]

Another parallel between Jean Froissart's presentation of John Ball's sermon and Luke's (or Q's) presentation of the Sermon on the Plain is that both presentations attempt to encapsulate the ideology and purpose of the relevant speaker; in other words, they are both presentations of a kind of

---

1. For a more detailed defense of this claim, see Allison, *Constructing Jesus,* 374–381.

ideological manifesto. Both of these "manifestos" (the Sermon on the Plain and John Ball's sermon) are also completely contingent on the historical context: they are speaking to real people living under real conditions of oppression and exploitation, and they are engaging with other ideologies that are likewise also historically contingent. However, both of these manifestos are appealing to, drawing on, and expressing, what the speaker considers to be higher truths (such as ideas of equality, morality, and so on).

One of the reasons that I posit this model is that the Sermon, as we will see, makes more sense when read as the teachings of an early first-century apocalyptic Jewish teacher in Galilee interacting with other Galilean Jews about issues that concern Galilean Jews of the early first century. The Sermon also posits and expresses an overarching ideology and worldview that informs its teachings and vision.

What I hope to do in this book is to analyze the Sermon on the Plain as it is recorded in Luke and attempt to contextualize it and to reconstruct its original meaning to its intended audience.

Before moving on, I would like to add a little note about why I chose to focus on the Sermon on the Plain found in thirty verses of Luke rather than the more famous Sermon on the Mount found in three chapters of Matthew. One reason is personal: there is much literature focusing on the Sermon on the Mount; while there is comparatively little focusing on the Sermon on the Plain, and I happened to slightly prefer the Sermon on the Plain, both aesthetically and in terms of the actual ethical material. Another is that among redaction critics, the tendency leans towards saying Luke's version maintains a less redacted and more original structure.[2] I love both the Sermon on the Plain and the Sermon on the Mount, but if I was forced to pick one—in terms of historical value and ethical force—I would likely go with the Sermon on the Plain. With that, let us look at the context of the Sermon.

---

2. Kloppenborg, *The formation of Q,* 171–172; Mack, *The Lost Gospel,* 188.

2

The Context

Historical Context

THE SERMON ON THE Plain was delivered as part of Jesus's ministry in Galilee.[1] During the time of Jesus, Galilee and Judea were under occupation by the Roman Empire and had been going through rather tumultuous times—politically, economically, and socially. Judea was conquered by Rome by Pompeii in 63 BCE, thus reducing the Hasmonean rulers to being vassals of Rome.[2] By the time Jesus was born, King Herod had replaced the Hasmoneans as the Roman vassal and ruler of Judea, Galilee, and Perea. King Herod secured his position of power with political maneuvering and brutality; he made sure that he controlled the high priesthood, replacing the Hasmonean high priest with one loyal to him,[3] and as he got older he killed any family member he suspected of too much ambition.[4] After Herod's death in 4 CE his kingdom was split between three of his sons: Philip got Iturea and Trachonitis, Antipas got Perea and Galilee (Jesus's home), and Archelaus got Judea, Samaria and Idumea. Only two years later however, Archelaus was dismissed and his territory was made a Roman province and placed directly under a prefect.[5] Within Galilee itself, the two

1. Bock, *The Theology of Luke and Acts*, 69–72.
2. Ferguson, *Backgrounds of Early Christianity*, 411–412.
3. Witherington III, *New Testament History*, 56–57.
4. Witherington III, *New Testament History*, 60.
5. Ferguson, *Backgrounds of Early Christianity*, 414–415.

major cities were Sepphoris and Tiberius—both built by Herod Antipas, and both built in Greco-Roman style.[6]

The economic situation under Herod and his successors was a mixed bag,[7] on the one hand it was a time of extraordinary economic development and urbanization;[8] on the other hand there was a rapidly growing class divide, with many people falling into destitution, especially the rural peasantry.[9] One reason for this was the increased taxation required for building projects, along with an increase of rent for land tenants and an increase of debt among the peasantry. As costs increased, more peasants would be forced to supplement their income through waged labor, and more would have to take on loans. The more loans one took the higher the risk of foreclosure, which resulted in more land ending up in the hands of the wealthy Herodian elite: those aristocratic families loyal to and tied to the Herodian dynasty.[10] The majority of the population—the peasantry—were either in a constant struggle to hold on to their land, while dealing with the increase of debt, tax, and rent; or were already among the landless poor and reduced to scraping a living together through wage labor or whatever means they had available.[11] As commercial activity increased, the value of land increased,

6. Horsley, "Jesus Movements and the Renewal of Israel," in Horsley, *A People's History of Christianity*, 35.

7. Much of the historical scholarship I rely on in this section uses social-scientific models and comparative studies (such as the macro-sociological analysis of various societies by Gerhard Lenski, James Scott's analysis of peasant societies, and the economic anthropology of Karl Polanyi) through which conditions are reconstructed using textual and archaeological data. One benefit of this methodology is that these social-scientific models provide the historian with the tools to extrapolate conditions from texts written by ancient authors who may have not been concerned with, or even aware of those conditions, as well as to interpret archaeological finds. For example, an ancient author may praise a ruler's urbanization and building projects while condemning the unruliness of the peasantry; using social-scientific models, a close reading of the text, and archaeological finds, the historian can model effects urbanization tends to have on agrarian societies, and model the general causes of peasant unrest in agrarian societies, to see if these models match the textual and archaeological data available.

8. Meyers and Chancey, *Alexander to Constantine: Archaeology of the Land of the Bible*, 51–52.

9. Herzog II, "Why Peasants Responded to Jesus," in Horsley, *A People's History of Christianity*, 50–51.

10. Horsley, "Jesus Movements and the Renewal of Israel," in Horsley, *A People's History of Christianity*, 35; Herzog II, "Why Peasants Responded to Jesus," in Horsley, *A People's History of Christianity*, 50–51; Oakman, *Jesus and the Peasants*, 24.

11. Freyne, "Galilee and Judea in the first century," in Mitchell and Young, *The Cambridge History of Christianity*, 42.

which made the acquisition of land through foreclosure or other means look ever more enticing to the rich.[12] The shift of wealth upwards to the Herodian aristocracy and the move to insecurity for much of the peasant class was a direct result of the political decision to build up Sepphoris and Tiberias.[13]

This is not to say that the peasantry was in desperate poverty, archeological digs have found that the average Galilean peasant maintained a decent standard of living, often through supplementing their farming with income from industry and trade.[14] It was however, a period of economic stratification and an economic shift,[15] in which many people were left feeling as though they had been left out of the growth, and felt increasingly as though they were in a precarious position as the land ownership became more and more centralized.[16] This economic shift in Galilee had a large effect on rural village life and the village communities.

Before we continue to talk about the economic realities in first-century Galilee. It would be helpful to make some broad observations on economics within ancient societies. Within any given society, one can differentiate between two realms of the economy: market and communal.[17] One major difference between the two realms is that in the communal realm the goods that circulate do so in the context of relationships held for their own sake; whereas in the market realm the relationships are formed, short term, in order to circulate goods for the sake of a certain project or for the sake of securing certain goods or services.[18] The base of the communal realm is the commons, which does not just consist of natural resources, but also of culture, tradition, and even sacred texts and objects. These commons are regulated by moral obligations within the community which come from different enforcement structures, either egalitarian or hierarchical (egalitarian enforcement could be for example, social ostracization; hierarchical

---

12. Oakman, *Jesus and the Peasants*, 169.

13. Freyne, "Galilee and Judea in the first century," in Mitchell and Young, *The Cambridge History of Christianity*, 45.

14. Aviam, "People, Land, Economy and Belief in First-Century Galilee and its Origins," in Fiensy and Hawkins, *The Galilean Economy in the time of Jesus*, 29.

15. McCollough, "City and Village in Lower Galilee," in Fiensy and Hawkins, *The Galilean Economy in the time of Jesus*, 71–72.

16. Freyne, *Galilee and Gospel*, 98.

17. Gudeman, *The Anthropology of the Economy*, 1.

18. Gudeman, *The Anthropology of the Economy*, 10.

enforcement could be for example, village elders).[19] In the context of Galilee, the communal realm included the Israelite tradition, along with the mutual obligations and Torah regulations that came along with that; as well as the traditional gift/mutual aid kinship economies that are common in pre-industrial village societies.[20]

In General, the introduction of taxation into pre-industrial societies does not just add a burden of taxation to society; it also brings in an increased commercialization. Since most ancient independent village economies consist of mostly subsistence farmers who more or less know each other, the general method of economic distribution is mutual aid and lending.[21] Once taxes get introduced there suddenly becomes a universal demand for the currency in which one must pay taxes, which in turn leads people to attempt to attain that currency by forming short-term market relationships, since they have to have that currency when the tax man comes or they will suffer repercussions.[22]

This ultimately creates markets where markets may not have existed before, since prior to the universal need for currency through taxation, mutual aid and lending to one another was much more efficient than barter due to the problem of the "double coincidence of wants" (if I have eggs and need milk, the chances that someone will happened to have extra milk and also need eggs at this very moment nearby are rather slim).[23] Not only is it more efficient; but mutual aid and sharing are crucial since those in the community rely on each other to survive.[24] So it is only with the proliferation and circulation of currency as the primary means of distributing goods and services that people can stop relying on the relationships they have within the community.[25] With the growth and centralization of a tax regime, the market realm becomes larger and larger and the community realm becomes smaller since the demand for currency is enforced by the sword and the communal relationships are not.

---

19. Gudeman, *The Anthropology of the Economy,* 27–28.

20. Gudeman, *The Anthropology of the Economy,* 86–89.

21. Graeber, *Debt,* 98–100.

22. Graeber, *Debt,* 49–50.

23. Graeber, *Debt,* 34–37.

24. Patterson, "Distribution and Redistribution," In Carrier, *A Handbook of Economic Anthropology,* 196–197.

25. Hann and Hart, *Economic Anthropology,* 94.

In other words, as the cost of living measured in money goes up (by increasing taxes, fees, or rents), so does the demand for money, which means less effort will go into maintaining the communal sphere of society and more will go into commercial activity to gain a monetary return. This is especially true in small village communities where social cohesion is maintained through trust, and where sharing is culturally enforced,[26] and where production is traditionally thought of as being for consumption rather than commercial activity.[27]

Returning to the context of first-century Galilee, we see a somewhat similar pattern played out. Although archaeological evidence shows a large increase in coinage during the Hasmonean period, indicating that a shift to a monetary economy began long before Jesus[28]—during Jesus's time it seems as though the money supply remained rather stable[29]—we do however see an increasing commercialization during the first century CE.[30] We see that even in the villages of first-century Galilee more luxury items were being traded,[31] and imported,[32] and they even developed new industries.[33] This is the upside of commercialization; the downside includes what we already mentioned: taxation, debt, and centralization of land to the elite, in other words, social inequality.

The growing economic insecurity and the redistribution upwards of land through debt instruments and foreclosures completely changed the nature of rural Galilean life and threatened to uproot many communities, forcing more to seek employment in the cities. Galilee had already become completely monetized and was increasingly commercialized, leaving behind the more communal structures, and the peasantry had no choice but to adapt.[34]

---

26. Graeber, *Debt*, 33–34.

27. Oakman, *Jesus and the Peasants*, 167.

28. Jensen, *Herod Antipas in Galilee*, 215.

29. Root, *First-Century Galilee*, 124–125.

30. Crossley, *Why Christianity Happened*, 43–45.

31. Aviam, "People, Land, Economy, and Belief in First-Century Galilee and its Origins," in Fiensy and Hawkins, *The Galilean Economy in the time of Jesus*, 28–29.

32. Edwards, "The Socio-Economic and Cultural Ethos of Lower Galilee in the First Century," in Levine, *The Galilee in Late Antiquity*, 60.

33. McCollough, "City and Village in Lower Galilee," in Fiensy and Hawkins, *The Galilean Economy in the time of Jesus*, 62.

34. Freyne, *Galilee and Gospel*, 103–104.

Once the communal realm became weakened and displaced by the market realm, the communities that the communal realm sustained became weaker and weaker; while market forces became stronger. This exacerbated the social divide between the city and the countryside, the rich and the poor.[35]

Of course, one should not get the idea that the introduction of urbanization introduced inequality and exploitation, it was there before; rather, it intensified it and took a traditional agrarian society and turned it into a commercialized one. One where land becomes a commodity that can be used to loan against, and where the aristocracy begins to get a taste for luxury and trade, requiring a larger surplus from the peasantry, which results in ever increasing land rents.[36] These large cities would also mean more mixing of classes, as peasants pushed into wage labor, or craftsmen wanting to make a living in the city, would come into contact with the urban elite and absentee landlords. It would also mean that the role of rural villages would be geared towards providing for the cities developing nearby.[37] One such village was Jesus's own Nazareth.

Of course, as we already mentioned, this does not mean that Galilee was necessarily materially poor, or even getting poorer; rather, it is the insecurity, the commercialization, and the perceived lack of control over one's future, and the class divide, that marked a shift in the social consciousness.

This shift led to a lot of resentment, resistance, and rebellion, as is often the case when a society begins to become part of a commercialized agrarian empire.[38] One pivotal example of this is a Galilean revolt that happened during Jesus's youth: the revolt of Judas of Galilee against the census of 6 CE. Augustus Caesar had sent out Quirinius to conduct a census of the region for the purpose of taxation. As a result, Judas of Galilee and a Pharisee named Saddok incited and led a resistance movement.[39] Josephus describes them this way:

> [Judas and Saddok] became zealous to draw them to a revolt, who both said that this taxation was no better than an introduction to slavery, and exhorted the nation to assert their liberty; as if they

35. Horsley, "Jesus Movements and the Renewal of Israel," in Horsley, *A People's History of Christianity*, 35; Meyers and Chancey, *Alexander to Constantine*, 120.

36. Crossley, *Why Christianity Happened*, 40–41.

37. Crossley, *Why Christianity Happened*, 44–45.

38. Crossley, *Why Christianity Happened*, 41.

39. Witherington III, *New Testament History*, 86–87.

could procure them happiness and security for what they possessed, and an assured enjoyment of a still greater good, which was that of the honor and glory they would thereby acquire for magnanimity. They also said that God would not otherwise be assisting to them, than upon their joining with one another in such councils as might be successful, and for their own advantage; and this especially, if they would set about great exploits, and not grow weary in executing the same; so men received what they said with pleasure, and this bold attempt proceeded to a great height. (Josephus, *A.J.*, 18.1.1 [Whiston])

He describes Judas the Galilean as the author of the "fourth sect," a "sect" which many claim was the intellectual forbearer of the Zealots[40] (who eventually led the revolt in the 60s CE that resulted in the destruction of the temple). He describes their ideology in this way:

These men agree in all other things with the Pharisaic notions; but they have an inviolable attachment to liberty, and say that God is to be their only Ruler and Lord. They also do not value dying any kinds of death, nor indeed do they heed the deaths of their relations and friends, nor can any such fear make them call any man lord. (Josephus, *A.J.*, 18.1.6)

Eventually Judas of Galilee was killed by the Romans and his followers were scattered (Acts 5:37). This revolt reflects the mindset of many in Galilee at the time: being under the taxation regime of Rome not only means the loss of freedom, but would also mean a lack of faithfulness to God, who is to be their only ruler and lord; and that to gain God's favor, they must resist. This revolt was not an outlier, it was an extreme example of the norm; both before and after Jesus's ministry, Galilee was full of unrest, riots, banditry, strikes, and anti-Roman and anti-Herodian prophetic movements.[41] For example, a few years after Jesus's ministry, the Roman Emperor Caligula had a statue of himself installed in the Jerusalem temple. The Galilean peasants responded by striking and refusing to plant crops, thus depriving the Romans and Herodians of taxes and rent. Luckily Caligula was assassinated soon after, preventing an escalation of the situation. Again, in this case,

---

40. Horsley, *Jesus and the Spiral of Violence*, 78–79.

41. Crossley, *Why Christianity Happened*, 46–47; 50–51; Freyne, "Galilee and Judea in the first century," in Mitchell and Young, *The Cambridge History of Christianity*, 46.

Josephus's historical works recount many such movements and disturbances in Judea, Galilee, and Perea. In some places he simply lists one after the other (Josephus, *A.J.*, 17.10.4–8; *J.W.*, 2.4.1–3).

just as in the protests of Judas of Galilee, the religious and economic are tied. In the case of Judas of Galilee, an economic act of Rome provoked a religiously inspired resistance; in the case of the strike, a religious offense provoked an economic response from the peasantry.[42] The connection between the religious and the economic is understandable given the fact that the communal realm of the economy contains within it the cultural commons—which in the case of Galilee included the Israelite tradition. When the moral obligations that the Galileans had with each other became threatened and replaced with market mechanisms, the communal realm, including the shared Israelite tradition, also became threatened.

Although there was economic legislation protecting debtors and the poor in the Jewish law code which was taken seriously,[43] different religious authorities found loopholes to dampen the effects of those laws; one example of such a loophole is the *Prozbul*, which we will discuss more later on in this book.[44] The shift of economic conditions affecting the poor, as well as the failure of the authorities to counteract the effects, resulted in a traditionalist backlash. Much of this backlash made use of the Jubilee and Sabbatical year legislations as eschatological symbols, and their use as symbols became more prominent in the first century BCE onward.[45]

One example of a prophetic resistance movement making use of Jewish symbolism around this time is that of Theudas who persuaded a lot of people to go with him to the Jordan river, where he said he would divide the river for an easy crossing (just like the dividing of the Red Sea by Moses and the Jordan River by Joshua). The result was that a cavalry unit attacked the gathering, killed Theudas, and brought his head to Jerusalem (Josephus, *A.J.*, 20.5.1). This example shows how seriously the authorities took even symbolic prophetic movements that drew from the Hebrew biblical tradition. These traditions, such as those Theudas was appealing to, threatened to give the people a narrative for liberation. If God rescued the Israelite slaves and brought them to the Promised Land, any sign that there was hope of something similar in Theudas's movement could lead a lot of

---

42. Horsley, "Jesus Movements and the Renewal of Israel," in Horsley, *A People's History of Christianity*, 25–26.

43. One example of this was the Sabbatical year law found in Deuteronomy 15, which we will discuss in a later chapter. We know from Josephus (*A.J.* 12.9.5; 13.8.1; 14.10.5–6; 14.16.2; 15.1.2, *J.W.* 1.2.4) that this legislation was taken seriously and followed.

44. Horsley, *Jesus and the Spiral of Violence*, 251–253.

45. Freyne, *Galilee and Gospel*, 109.

people to refuse to accept the current order—in fact, they may even feel that it is their religious duty to oppose it.[46]

Galilee, although separated and culturally distinct from Judea, retained a strong Jewish identity, and the archeological evidence show that the Galilean population generally followed Torah regulations and considered themselves part of the Israelite tradition.[47] Many anthropologists distinguish between "great tradition" and "little tradition;" in the case of Galilee the former would be the textual tradition controlled by the scribal class and priests, the latter would be more oral and based in villages. In the case of Galilee, the two traditions generally came from the same sources: the biblical narrative. The "little tradition" of the villagers would shape the biblical narrative in the sense of selecting and reciting the tradition in a way that was relevant to their own life situation, and in a way that sustained their culture.[48] Jesus's ministry reflects a "little tradition" background.[49] This is seen in the material of his teachings and parables with their themes of debt, employment, agriculture, dispossession, money, and so on; as well as his use of the biblical sources within a "little tradition" framework—a very obvious example of this is the figure of Abraham in the parable of the rich man and Lazarus in Luke 16:19–31.[50]

It is within this "little tradition" that the Sermon on the Plain is embedded. Jesus is talking from the perspective of someone belonging to the downwardly mobile peasant class; someone who may have actually worked in Sepphoris and saw the divide first hand between rich and poor, city and countryside, and someone who experienced the economic anxiety that people in that class had. Jesus is described in Mark 6:3 as a "carpenter," or the "son of a carpenter" in Matthew 13:55. The term translated "carpenter" (τέκτων) is probably better rendered "woodworker," or perhaps, so as to avoid thinking anachronistically, simply "builder."[51] As a builder, Jesus was

46. Horsley, "Jesus Movements and the Renewal of Israel," in Horsley, *A People's History of Christianity*, 29–30.

47. Dunn, *Christianity in the making Volume 1*, 294–296.

48. Herzog II, "Why Peasants Responded to Jesus," in Horsley, *A People's History of Christianity*, 52–53.

49. Herzog II, "Why Peasants Responded to Jesus," in Horsley, *A People's History of Christianity*, 55.

50. Herzog II, "Why Peasants Responded to Jesus," in Horsley, *A People's History of Christianity*, 58–60. This pericope is only found in Luke.

51. Levine, "Introduction," in Levine, Allison, Crossan, in Levine, Allison, Crossan, *The Historical Jesus in Context*, 19; Reed, "Archaeological Contributions to the Study of

part of the peasant class—in that he was part of the rural agrarian economy on the level of a relatively stable laborer, this context is especially reflected in his parables[52]—not quite destitute, but still poor.[53] Likely, Jesus would have grown up seeing his peers fall into destitution—forced into precarious migrant labor, banditry, or beggardry—as financial pressures increased.

Unlike scholars such as John P. Meier, I believe it is rather likely that Jesus traveled to large nearby cities, such as Sepphoris, for work—despite Jesus not being recorded as visiting such larger nearby cities during his ministry[54]—there are hints that prior to his ministry he may have worked in those cities.[55] Sepphoris was only six and a half kilometers (four miles) from Nazareth, and was, as we have already seen, going through extensive construction and expansion during Jesus's youth. It would be surprising if someone working as a woodworker in Nazareth would not have taken advantage of the employment opportunities found in a large city close by. Another clue that Jesus might have worked in Sepphoris is that Sepphoris was predominantly Hellenistic in character; as we will see later, it does seem that Jesus interacts, even if only in a general and broad way, with Hellenistic ethical thought in the Sermon on the Plain.[56] We get hints of Jesus's vague familiarity with Hellenistic culture elsewhere: such as his knowledge of Hellenistic government and patronage.[57] Jesus is recorded as understanding economics enough, including currency exchange and

---

Jesus and the Gospels," in Levine, Allison and Crossan, *The Historical Jesus in Context*, 50.

52. Meier, *A Marginal Jew: Volume 1*, 279–280; Oakman, *Jesus and the Peasants*, 172. Many of Jesus's parables reflect the viewpoint of a peasant, and many of those reflect that of a peasant working on a large estate, such as those on the Esdraelon Plain near Jesus's hometown of Nazareth. Even though his occupation could classify him as an artisan, there is an early tradition tying Jesus's family to an agrarian lifestyle (Eusebius, Church History, 3.20); his hometown and his parables also point to a peasant socialization.

53. Meier, *A Marginal Jew: Volume 1*, 282.

54. Meier, *A Marginal Jew: Volume 1*, 284.

55. Sean Freyne supposes that the reason Jesus avoided those cities during his ministry, is because of his conscious opposition to the values those cities represented, a supposition that assumes that Jesus was familiar with those cities. Freyne, *Jesus, A Jewish Galilean*, 144–145.

56. Witherington III, *New Testament History*, 111.

57. Mark 10:42; Luke 22:25; Matthew 20:25—only Luke's version includes a reference to patronage (εὐεργέτης), however given the context in Mark and Matthew being about "greatness" and "service," it seems likely that the concept of patronage is implicit in Mark's and Matthew's version as well.

market pricing to know when people were being cheated,[58] and he seemed to hold strong opinions on what "people of the nations" do as opposed to what righteous people ought to do.[59] Of course we have no proof either way, but the fact that he does not visit Sepphoris or Tiberius during his ministry should not count against him having worked there in his youth, since that could easily be explained by Jesus simply choosing an audience he would believe to be receptive to his message. The fact that no visit is mentioned in the gospels should not count against him having worked there either since almost nothing about his pre-ministry life is mentioned. Given this I think we can say that it is rather likely that Jesus did spend some time in Sepphoris during his youth to work—and that this experience likely had an impact on his ministry.

Literary Context

The book in which the Sermon on the Plain is found is Luke, which itself is part of the larger work of Luke-Acts. To understand the Sermon on the Plain we have to understand its place within the Luke-Acts work, how it functions within that work, and what the general ideology is behind that work, and how the Sermon contributes to that ideology. Of course one must be careful here not to go too far in interpreting the Sermon purely from the standpoint of the ideology of the author of Luke-Acts—Luke used many sources in his gospel[60]—and it seems that he kept to the sources relatively faithfully,[61] and he tends to hold to the sequence of his sources and avoid conflation.[62] The Sermon on the Plain almost certainly comes from one of his sources,[63] therefore it is possible to exegete the Sermon independently,

---

58. Mark 11:15–18; Matthew 21:12–14; Luke 19:45–46; John 2:13–17.

59. Mark 10:42; Luke 22:25; Matthew 20:25; Luke 12:29–31; Matthew 6:31–33; Matthew 6:7; Matthew 5:47.

60. Fitzmyer, *The Gospel According to Luke I–IX*, 63. See Luke 1:1–4.

61. Fitzmyer, *The Gospel According to Luke I–IX*, 107–108.

62. Derrenbacker, *Ancient Compositional Practices and the Synoptic Problem*, 261–263.

63. The majority of New Testament scholars, as of now, accept the two-source hypothesis in which Luke and Matthew use Mark and "Q" as sources, "Q" usually being the pericopes that are not found in Mark, but that Matthew and Luke have in common. I will not take a position on the synoptic problem here. What I think can be said however, without too much controversy, is that Luke 6:20–49 derives from a pre-Lukan source; be that source a sayings gospel such as "Q," an oral tradition, Matthew, or even as Alan

not merely as an aspect of the Luke-Acts work. If one is inclined to believe (as many scholars do) that the Sermon on the Mount (Matthew 5–7) and the Sermon on the Plain (Luke 6:20–49) derive from the same source, it is likely that the Sermon on the Plain is closer to that original source; some reasons for this are that Luke's version is shorter and lacks many redactional features that various scholars have detected in Matthew.[64]

That being said, understanding how the Sermon fits into Luke's telling of the story of Jesus of Nazareth and the movement he spawned can help us to situate the Sermon and its message within the narrative itself and how it functioned as part of the ministry of Jesus and the life of the early Christian community.

Luke-Acts is a work of ancient biography/history, not a modern "scientific" historiography—a genre which often claims to attempt to be objective—but rather ancient history, which is often didactic in nature: it has a message to present.[65] That does not mean that the ancient historian is inventing fantasy to present a message; rather, this historian is taking sources, written, oral, or eye-witnesses, and creating a narrative that highlights his message. [66] The message of Luke-Acts is primarily kerygmatic: the work is a proclamation of Jesus's death and resurrection as the means of salvation. Salvation here means salvation from the ruling class and the earthly powers,[67] from Satan and wicked spirits,[68] from sickness, and even death,[69]—ultimately all of these are a part of salvation from sin.[70] Luke-Acts begins with the story of the proclaimer of the Kingdom of God in Luke, and then this proclaimer becomes the proclaimed in Acts.[71] Jesus's *kerygma*

Garrow has suggested in "An Extant Instance of 'Q'" in the Journal for New Testament Studies 62.3, July, 2016: the *Didache*. My own position is that the Sermon on the Plain we find in Luke is derived from a source which itself represents a paraphrase of the actual teachings of the historical Jesus—as I will point out later, much of the Sermon fits in rather well with the context of the historical Jesus.

64. Allison, *Constructing Jesus*, 310–311; Horsley, *Jesus and the Spiral of Violence*, 260.

65. Bock, *The Theology of Luke and Acts*, 45; 47.

66. Evans, *Saint Luke*, 45–46.

67. Bock, *The Theology of Luke and Acts*, 228–229.

68. Bock, *The Theology of Luke and Acts*, 250.

69. Bock, *The Theology of Luke and Acts*, 230.

70. Bock, *The Theology of Luke and Acts*, 237.

71. Fitzmyer, *The Gospel According to Luke I–IX*, 146.

is best illustrated in his reading of Isaiah at the synagogue of Nazareth,[72] where he makes his inaugural declaration:[73]

> "The Spirit of the Lord is upon me, because he has anointed me to bring good news to the poor.
>
> He has sent me to proclaim release to the captives and recovery of sight to the blind, to let the oppressed go free, to proclaim the year of the Lord's favor."
>
> And he rolled up the scroll, gave it back to the attendant, and sat down. The eyes of all in the synagogue were fixed on him. Then he began to say to them, "Today this scripture has been fulfilled in your hearing." (Luke 4:18–21 [NRSV])

This declaration mixes Isaiah 61:1–2 and Isaiah 58:6. Isaiah 61 is a song of deliverance for the exiled Jews in Babylon; the imagery used is based on the Jubilee legislation, which was a kind of legislated regular revolution in which the land was redistributed, the debts were cancelled, and the slaves freed. Isaiah 58 is a message of judgment against the people for not keeping their obligation to care for the poor—it prioritizes the message of care for the poor over ritual practices such as fasting—and Isaiah 58 uses similar imagery in describing a release, and also brings into play the Sabbath legislation. In applying these scriptures to himself Jesus is declaring that he is the one who will fulfill these promises.[74] For Luke, Jesus's declaration was, in one sense, fulfilled in his lifetime, as we see with the claim that this scripture has been fulfilled today.[75] The declaration Luke is presenting is that with Jesus, comes a completely new era, an era of salvation, or liberation; and that this era is part of God's plan, the fulfillment of God's word.[76] In this sense we can say that although Luke-Acts is a biography of Jesus and a history of the Christian movement, the main character is God, since it is his will being fulfilled in the life of Jesus and the history of the Christian movement.[77] There are many indications in Luke that there is an expectation of the coming of an eschatological "Kingdom of God." This is indicated

---

72. Fitzmyer, *The Gospel According to Luke I–IX*, 149–150.

73. This pericope is only found in Luke.

74. Bock, *The Theology of Luke and Acts*, 162.

75. Fitzmyer, *The Gospel According to Luke I–IX*, 150.

76. Fitzmyer, *The Gospel According to Luke I–IX*, 133–244.

77. Bock, *The Theology of Luke and Acts*, 99–100.

in Jesus's sending out of the seventy disciples in Luke 10:1–16[78] along with the message he gives them which we read in verse 9:

> The kingdom of God has come near to you. (Luke 10:9)

We also get many indications in the book of Acts of a coming eschatological age, for example in Peter's first speech in Jerusalem:

> 'In the last days it will be, God declares, that I will pour out my Spirit upon all flesh, and your sons and your daughters shall prophesy, and your young men shall see visions, and your old men shall dream dreams.
>
> Even upon my slaves, both men and women, in those days I will pour out my Spirit; and they shall prophesy.
>
> And I will show portents in the heaven above and signs on the earth below, blood, and fire, and smoky mist.
>
> The sun shall be turned to darkness and the moon to blood, before the coming of the Lord's great and glorious day.
>
> Then everyone who calls on the name of the Lord shall be saved.' (Acts 2:17–21)

So we really have two proclamations in the Luke-Acts *kerygma*: The proclamation that salvation, release, and liberation had taken place—which Jesus proclaimed, and which the *ecclesia* proclaimed as being accomplished in Jesus,[79]—as well as the coming *eschaton* proclaimed both by Jesus and the *ecclesia*.[80] This can all be summed up by the main theme of the Luke-Acts work: The Kingdom of God, which is both coming, and already in place.[81] This double declaration is key to understanding Luke—it is neither a case of the Kingdom declaration simply being the creation of a new movement, neither is it a declaration of something to come which one can only wait for; rather, it is the declaration of a new age already visible here with the ministry of Jesus and the communities growing out of it which are part of what will ultimately be the eschatological end of history: the full Kingdom of God with eternal life, resurrection, and the possession of the earth by the righteous.[82] One way to refer to this double concept of the Kingdom

---

78. Fitzmyer, *The Gospel According to Luke I–IX*, 146. Verses 1–12 are only found in Luke.

79. Fitzmyer, *The Gospel According to Luke I–IX*, 186; Evans, *Saint Luke*, 98.

80. Fitzmyer, *The Gospel According to Luke I–IX*, 232–233; Evans, *Saint Luke*, 98.

81. For example, compare Luke 21:31; 10:11 with Luke 11:20; 17:21. Fitzmyer, *The Gospel According to Luke I–IX*, 154–155.

82. Evans, *Saint Luke*, 64; Bock, *The Theology of Luke and Acts*, 105–106.

is "already and not yet," it is already here but it is not yet completed.[83] This Kingdom of God reflects the idea of God being in control of history and that his people would be saved from the things that torment them; such as violence, danger, oppression, evil, and sin. This concept is rooted in the Hebrew bible and beyond in the Jewish tradition. [84] The theme of the promises of God, recorded in the Hebrew bible, being fulfilled in Jesus, is included in the *kerygma* of the Kingdom of God;[85] the idea being that the Hebrew bible records promises that are fulfilled in Jesus: in what he does; and that what he does and what happens to him is necessary for the sake of God's purpose.[86] For Luke, the *kerygma* is not a break with Israel's history; but rather it is a proclamation for Israel, that Jesus is Israel's messiah—he is the fulfillment of promises to Israel; and when Gentiles are included in that fulfillment, it is because their inclusion is rooted in the promises to Israel.[87]

Two of the most important scriptures from the Hebrew Bible in relation to the Kingdom of God and the figure of the messiah are found in Psalms 110 and Daniel 7. Psalms 110:1 and Daniel 7:13–14 are combined together in two of the most important events in the Luke-Acts work. The first is Jesus's trial in Luke 22:69, where he answers the chief priests and scribes questioning him about his status as Christ by saying "But from now on the Son of Man will be seated at the right hand of the power of God." The second is Stephen's stoning in Acts 7:56, where Stephen sees the son of man standing at the right hand of God. Prior to Jesus's trial we have the son of man put in an eschatological context where Jesus is predicting the destruction of the temple, the gentile times, and the coming redemption; and in Luke 21:27 he says the son of man will be "coming on a cloud with power and great glory." These two events, as well as the allusions prior to Jesus's trial, place Psalms 110:1 and Daniel 7:13–14 at the center of Luke's understanding of the messiahship.

Psalm 110 is a song promising the destruction of the enemies of the King of Israel, Daniel 7 is a vision of a heavenly "son of man" figure who rules the entire world on behalf of God. Luke portrays Jesus both as the

---

83. Bock, *The Theology of Luke and Acts*, 143.

84. Fitzmyer, *The Gospel According to Luke I–IX*, 155.

85. Bock, *The Theology of Luke and Acts*, 131.

86. Bock, *The Theology of Luke and Acts*, 140–141.

87. Bock, *The Theology of Luke and Acts*, 289.

King, ruling on God's behalf,[88] as well as this "son of man" figure.[89] Both of these portrayals of Jesus are related to his historic title of "the Christ" or "the Messiah," which is a title Luke puts a lot of weight on, while using the term in a very theologically sensitive way.[90] For Luke, Jesus's messiahship involved Jesus inheriting the Davidic Kingship—except in a larger eschatological way than perhaps anticipated—he is not only the King of Israel; but ultimately the King of God's Kingdom which involves being the "son of man" of Daniel 7, bringing about divine judgment.[91] However, Jesus is a different kind of king: he is the King who suffers in order to be the King—he is completely powerless and dishonored, it is through this very state that he is made the glorified King, the anointed one.[92] This semi-paradoxical reversing of the concept of power, claiming that real kingship and glorification comes from the bottom—from suffering and degradation—is a very strong theme in Luke and is strongly related to Luke's notion of social justice.[93]

Luke, more so than any other gospel, has a strong emphasis on social justice: the raising up of the poor and powerless, and the bringing down of the rich and powerful.[94] We have already seen this emphasis in his mission statement given at the synagogue of Nazareth in Luke 4:18–19.[95] Some of the strongest passages in this regard are Mary's Magnificat prayer (Luke 1:47–55),[96] the blessings and woes of the Sermon (Luke 6:20–26, these we will look closer at later), and the story of the rich man and Lazarus (Luke 16:19–31).[97] The main idea in these passages is that God favors the poor and will raise them up, and that he will bring down the rich. Along with this somewhat radical, and perhaps eschatological,[98] attitude, is a social justice more focused on ethics rather than on the actions of God. These ethics are not individual, but based in community: they function as a way to build a

---

88. Fitzmyer, *The Gospel According to Luke I–IX*, 215–216.

89. Fitzmyer, *The Gospel According to Luke I–IX*, 210–211.

90. Evans, *Saint Luke*, 73–74.

91. Evans, *Saint Luke*, 81; Bock, *The Theology of Luke and Acts*, 180–181.

92. Evans, *Saint Luke*, 73–76.

93. Evans, *Saint Luke*, 100–101.

94. Fitzmyer, *The Gospel According to Luke I–IX*, 247.

95. This pericope is only found in Luke.

96. This pericope is only found in Luke.

97. This pericope is only found in Luke.

98. Bock, *The Theology of Luke and Acts*, 101.

Godly community dedicated to Jesus.[99] The ethics are found in John the Baptist's teachings (Luke 3:7–14),[100] the ethics portion of the Sermon on the Plain (Luke 6:27–38, these we will look closer at later), the story of the rich fool (Luke 12:16–26),[101] the parable of the dinner party (14:15–24), the story of the rich young ruler (Luke 18:18–25), the story of Zacchaeus (19:1–10),[102] and so on. As we see in Jesus's proclamation in Luke 4:18–19, the social justice aspect of Jesus's preaching was not separate from his Kingdom *kerygma*, it was rather the direct result of the Kingdom of God coming and the community of disciples awaiting the *eschaton*.[103] This community was one that was kerygmatic: declaring the good news of the Kingdom; as well as communal: living out the ethics of the kingdom in the here and now.[104]

---

99. Bock, *The Theology of Luke and Acts*, 147.

100. Verses 10–14 are only found in Luke.

101. Verses 19–21 are only found in Luke.

102. Verses 1–9 are only found in Luke.

103. Evans, *Saint Luke*, 99.

104. Bock, *The Theology of Luke and Acts*, 312.

The Sermon on the Plain

The Sermon on the Plain in Luke 6 can be broken into three sections:

1. The blessings and woes (verses 20–26)
2. The Ethics (verses 27–38)
3. The Parables (verses 39–49)

The first section sets up the programmatic background of the Sermon and the general worldview through which the rest of the Sermon is to be heard. The second section is the meat of the Sermon, which lays out the ethics being taught by Jesus. The third section is a series of parables that highlight the need for action and that give practical wisdom.[105] Although Luke 6:20–49 is known as the Sermon on the Plain, it should not necessarily be thought of as a sermon in the sense of a religious discourse alone; it is much more than that. As we will see, the Sermon on the Plain functions more like a manifesto—laying out an eschatological program that ideologically dismantles the existing social order, laying out a vision for a new kind of communal life, and a call to change the structure of social relationships. The Sermon on the Plain is, in many ways, the summation of Jesus's message: the *kerygma* of the Kingdom of God and the ethical demands of that *kerygma*.

As to the historicity of the Sermon, and its going back to the historical Jesus, we will see that much of the Sermon is multiply attested outside of the synoptic tradition, we will also see that it fits very well with the general record we have of the historical Jesus, and his context. As you read the Sermon, you will notice certain patterns—such as the rhythm of the blessings and woes, or the alliteration, parallelism, balance, and repetition of the ethics, or the vividness of the parables—that point to an oral origin which was committed to memory by early Christian communities.[106] Dale Allison, in arguing for the historicity of Luke 6:27–42, writes:

> Various observations on the preceding pages, above all the thematic coherence of the discourse and its consistent interaction with Lev 19 and associated exegetical tradition, point in the same direction, or rather to the same person.
>
> . . .

105. Marshall, *The Gospel of Luke*, 243.
106. Allison, *Constructing Jesus*, 374–377.

> We gain no explanatory advantage by assigning Q 6:27–42 to
> a contemporary of Jesus rather than to Jesus himself—so we may,
> if we wish, surmise that he was its primary author.[107]

Although Dale Allison argues primarily for the historicity of Luke 6:27–42, I hope to demonstrate that the blessings and woes also fit within the "thematic coherence of the discourse" and also likely belong to the original set of teachings. I am additionally of the opinion that verses 43–49 also, at least have a reasonable probability, of belonging to the original set of teachings.

However, my primary goal is not the historical reconstruction of any speech of the historical Jesus, but rather a historical reconstruction of its message, and what the Sermon would mean to those who heard it.

107. Allison, *Constructing Jesus*, 380.

3

The Blessings and Woes

The Vision of Jesus

STARTING WITH THE BLESSINGS and woes, we see four blessings along with four concomitant woes. The term often translated "blessed" (μακάριοι), can be translated "happy" (which is how I translate the term), "fortunate," or any term that conveys the idea of inner happiness;[1] and in the blessings and woes of the Sermon on the Plain, it conveys an exaltation of people who have this state of inner happiness due to good things happening to them.[2] The literary form of pronouncing someone blessed is often referred to as a "*macarism*," and this form was common in Greek literature, often applying the *macarism* to the gods.[3] It was also used in the Jewish context, often referring to the good fortune that reflected God's favor.[4] The term translated "woe" (οὐαὶ) is used abundantly in the LXX, where it can imply a threat, and where it can convey displeasure, grief, or pain.[5] Looking at the structure of the blessings and woes in the Sermon on the Plain, we see that the last blessing and the last woe seem to not fit well with the first three blessings

---

1. BDAG, μακάριος.

2. Fitzmyer, *The Gospel According to Luke I–IX*, 632–633.

3. Evans, *Saint Luke*, 328–329. For example: *Hymn to Ares*, 8.1; *Hymn to Apollo*, 3.10; *Hymn to Poseidon*, 22.1; Aeschylus, *Suppliant Woman*, 525; Aeschylus, *Agamemnon*, 505; Plutarch, *Quaestiones Romanae*, 207.

4. For example: Sirach 14:20; 26:1; Psalms 1:1; 127:3–5; Job 29:10–11 (LXX).

5. Fitzmyer, *The Gospel According to Luke I–IX*, 636.

and woes. Looking at the blessings and woes, we immediately notice the rhythm of the text. The first three blessings read:[6]

Μακάριοι οἱ πτωχοί, ὅτι ὑμετέρα ἐστὶν ἡ βασιλεία τοῦ θεοῦ.

How happy are the destitute, because the Kingdom of God is YOURS.

μακάριοι οἱ πεινῶντες νῦν, ὅτι χορτασθήσεσθε.

How happy are the ones hungering now, because YOU will be made full.

μακάριοι οἱ κλαίοντες νῦν, ὅτι γελάσετε.

How happy are the ones weeping now, because YOU will laugh.

And the first three woes read:

οὐαὶ ὑμῖν τοῖς πλουσίοις, ὅτι ἀπέχετε τὴν παράκλησιν ὑμῶν.

Nevertheless, Woe to YOU, the rich, because YOU are receiving YOUR comfort.

οὐαὶ ὑμῖν, οἱ ἐμπεπλησμένοι νῦν, ὅτι πεινάσετε.

Woe to YOU, the ones who have been filled now; because YOU will hunger.

οὐαί, οἱ γελῶντες νῦν, ὅτι πενθήσετε καὶ κλαύσετε.

Woe to the ones laughing now, because YOU will mourn and weep.

All three blessings roughly match up rhythmically with their three concomitant woes (give or take one or two syllables), and they all match each other in form: μακάριοι οἱ + plural substantive, followed by a single-part ὅτι-clause. All three blessings and woes also focus on socio-economic standings: the poor verses the rich, the hungry verses the full, and those who weep and mourn—which is not strictly speaking a socio-economic category but rather the outwards sign of loss or calamity[7], in the Lukan context due to oppression[8]—verses those who laugh scornfully and disdainfully (which is often how the term γελνῶ is used in Jewish literature).[9]

6. All English quotations of Luke 6:20–49 will be from my own translation of those verses, which can be found in full starting on page 139 of this book.

7. Arnal, "Why Q Failed," in Matthews, *Redescribing Christian Origins,* 76–77.

8. Fitzmyer, *The Gospel According to Luke I–IX,* 632–634.

9. Tuckett, *Q and the History of Early Christianity,* 224–225. See also the use of γελνῶ in the LXX Greek translation of Genesis 17:17; 18:12–15, 2 Kings 19:21; Job 9:23; 22:19; Nehemiah 2:19; Psalms 21(22):8(7); 79(80):7(6); Isaiah 37:22.

What we have in these three blessings and woes is a reversal based on opposite classes: the underclass is blessed while the privileged class receives "woe." The blessings are presented in the third person plural, meaning that the underclass is an abstract third person group; however, the ὅτι-clauses are all in the second person plural, meaning once the third person group is established, the speaker then addresses that group personally. The first two woes address their audience directly using the second person plural pronoun—giving them a more direct, almost accusatory, feel—and all the ὅτι-clauses are in the second person plural.

The first blessing and the first woe deal with the current state of affairs that exists in the present age (the poor and the rich), contrasting that state of affairs with the state of affairs in the coming age. They do this using the present tense, as though the coming age is already assured: the poor already have the Kingdom of God, and the rich have their comfort (implying that their comfort will end). The second and third blessing and woe are slightly different in that they contrast the state of hungering and weeping "now" (emphasizing the present state of affairs) with that of being filled and laughing in the future (using the future tense); and the state of being filled, and scornfully and proudly laughing now, with that of hungering, mourning, and weeping in the future. The term πτωχοί (which is often translated as "poor," but which I have translated as "destitute"[10]) refers to the economically destitute, and are treated by Luke as a specific class favored by God and the group to which the Gospel is addressed.[11] The first blessing and woe sets up the two opposing classes—the destitute, or the truly poor, and the rich—and assigns their different roles in the Kingdom: the Kingdom is for the poor, whereas the rich get their comfort in the present age. The second and third blessings and woes describe the position of these two groups, both in the present and in the future when the Kingdom takes over: the poor hunger and weep now but will not in the future; whereas the rich are filled and are laughing now but will not be in the future. The second and third blessings are explained by the first one: we know that the Kingdom

10. According to the BDAG Lexicon, the primary meaning of πτωχος is one who is "dependent on others for support" (BDAG, πτωχος); this definition is captured by the term "destitute" much better than the term "poor," since "poor" can include those who may be economically able to care for themselves while having very little in the way of possessions.

11. Bock, *The Theology of Luke and Acts,* 202; 352–353; 355–356.

already belongs to the poor, which is why they will be made full and laugh. These blessings and woes are all eschatological in nature.[12]

The last blessing reads:

> μακάριοί ἐστε ὅταν μισήσωσιν ὑμᾶς οἱ ἄνθρωποι καὶ ὅταν ἀφορίσωσιν ὑμᾶς καὶ ὀνειδίσωσιν καὶ ἐκβάλωσιν τὸ ὄνομα ὑμῶν ὡς πονηρὸν ἕνεκα τοῦ υἱοῦ τοῦ ἀνθρώπου·

> How happy YOU are whenever people hate YOU, and when they separate from YOU, and when they revile YOU and cast out YOUR name as wicked on account of the Son of Man.

> χάρητε ἐν ἐκείνῃ τῇ ἡμέρᾳ καὶ σκιρτήσατε, ἰδοὺ γὰρ ὁ μισθὸς ὑμῶν πολὺς ἐν τῷ οὐρανῷ· κατὰ αὐτὰ γὰρ ἐποίουν τοῖς προφήταις οἱ πατέρες αὐτῶν.

> Rejoice in that day and leap for joy, because look, YOUR reward in heaven is great—for their fathers were doing these things against the prophets.

And its concomitant woe reads:

> οὐαὶ ὅταν ὑμᾶς καλῶς εἴπωσιν πάντες οἱ ἄνθρωποι·

> Woe when all people may speak well of YOU,

> κατὰ τὰ αὐτὰ γὰρ ἐποίουν τοῖς ψευδοπροφήταις οἱ πατέρες αὐτῶν.

> because their fathers were doing these things to the false prophets.

The fourth blessing does not match up at all with the woe rhythmically and the structure of the fourth blessing and woe does not match up with the structure of the first three. In the fourth blessing and woe we do not see any economic class, or any abstract group being addressed; rather, we see "YOU"—the second person plural without qualification, the entire audience, constituting a group attached to the "Son of Man"[13] (likely referring to the followers of Jesus)—and "people" or "everybody." The blessing and woe is not distributed to the two different groups, but rather distributed to the group attached to the Son of Man according to how they are treated by the "people/everybody" group. How the blessed ones are treated is that they

---

12. Evans, *Saint Luke*, 330; 333.

13. This is a clear reference to the "son of man" figure introduced in Daniel 7:13–14, and theorized about in popular Second Temple apocalyptic literature such as 1 Enoch.

are excluded, likely referring to being excluded from synagogues,[14] and have their name rejected on account of the son of man.

In the first three blessings and woes, the blessings and woes are distributed according to class, and the outcome is more or less set in stone: the underclass is getting the blessing, and the privileged class is getting the woe, end of story. In the fourth blessing and woe, we see how the "Son of Man" group is being treated in the subjunctive form, implying contingency. So, whether or not the "Son of Man" group receives a woe or a blessing depends on how the "people/everybody" group treats them. How the "people/everybody" group treats the "Son of Man" group also seems to depend on the actions and integrity of the "Son of Man" group, we see this clearly in the "κατὰ τὰ αὐτὰ γὰρ ἐποίουν" statements. The prophets were treated poorly by the fathers of the "people/everybody" group, whereas the false prophets were treated well, therefore if you are being treated poorly that is a sign that you are like the prophets, and thus in line for happiness, or blessedness; whereas if you are treated well, that is a sign that you are like the false prophets, and thus in line for a woe. The reference to the prophets reflects a tradition that had already developed in Judaism that portrayed the prophets as being persecuted.[15]

To explain this difference (along with other issues in the Q material) many Q scholars have proposed various stages of redaction in the Q material. For example, John Kloppenborg and Burton Mack divide the Q material into three stages of redaction, Q1, Q2, and Q3.[16] Q1 is thought of as belonging to the earliest writings of the followers of Jesus, where Jesus is a moral teacher. Q2 is thought of as being a second stage of redaction where issues involving group dynamics and conflicts with the outside world are addressed, as well as introducing an apocalyptic vision, and Q3 is thought of as being the last stage of redaction where Jesus is seen as the son of God.[17]

According to Burton Mack's and other's reconstruction, the first three blessings[18] are presented as being part of the Q1 material. Jesus here is sim-

---

14. Fitzmyer, *The Gospel According to Luke I–IX*, 635; Evans, *Saint Luke*, 331.

15. Evans, *Saint Luke*, 332.

16. Kloppenborg, *The formation of Q*, 96–100; Mack, *The Lost Gospel*, 44–49; 203–205.

17. Mack, *The Lost Gospel*, 45–47; 131–132; 160–161; 173–174.

18. Many Q theorists do not include the woes in their reconstructions of Q, although this is not unanimous, for example John Kloppenborg and Heinz Schürmann do include the woes. However, my argument for the inclusion of the fourth blessing in the original text of Q does not depend on the inclusion of the woes in the original text. I do, however, side with Kloppenborg and Schürmann in believing the woes are original and will

ply presenting a worldview, this serves a programmatic function for what follows in the rest of the Sermon, which is usually assigned to Q1.[19] The last blessing however, is presented as being part of the Q2 material due to its assumption of an "in group," and due to its assumption of a conflict with outside groups, as well as its introduction of the apocalyptic "Son of Man." The last blessing also includes an imperative with a motive clause and includes the idea of an eschatological reward (rather than just a reversal), which is a further reason it is presented as being a later addition. [20]

I do not think that positing the fourth blessing as a later redaction is at all necessary, and I believe that more sense can be made of the Sermon if we take all the blessings as a single block. One problem with the fourth-blessing-as-a-later-redaction framework is that the first three blessings and woes do not actually serve any programmatic function to what follows.

According to Mack's Q reconstruction, the rest of the Sermon on the Plain belongs to the Q1 material and thus follows the first three blessings,[21] this creates a problem in that the first three blessings, in and of themselves, do not actually fit with the rest of the material in the Sermon on the Plain; they do not set the stage for the Sermon on the Plain. These first three blessings are basically an eschatological reversal, and as we have seen in the first blessing, the use of the present tense implies that its reality is already set; the second two blessings' use of the future tense implies that the results are forthcoming.[22] The rest of the Sermon on the Plain however, is almost entirely made up of ethical injunctions, ethical injunctions that are communal in nature and often assume persecution, the entire point of the rest of the Sermon, is to provide a set of communal ethics in light of a hostile world.[23]

The blessings work as an eschatological reversal,[24] however, there is nothing connecting that reversal to the ethical framework that follows;

---

provide reasons for this position later on.

19. Arnal, "Why Q Failed," in Matthews, *Redescribing Christian Origins,* 75; Kloppenborg, *The formation of Q,* 189–190. John Kloppenborg accepts the early unity of the four blessings and woes (at least by the time they were united with the rest of the Sermon that follows), only omitting 6:23c "for their fathers were doing these things against the prophets" as a later redaction.

20. Arnal, "Why Q Failed," in Matthews, *Redescribing Christian Origins,* 77; Mack, *The Lost Gospel,* 138; 144–145; Kloppenborg, *The formation of Q,* 172–173.

21. Mack, *The Lost Gospel,* 73–74.

22. Dunn, *Christianity in the making Volume 1,* 413.

23. Dunn, *Christianity in the making Volume 1,* 586–588.

24. Fitzmyer, *The Gospel According to Luke I–IX,* 630.

the rest of the Sermon has no poor/rich class dichotomy, nor is there any eschatological reversal, in fact, there is almost no eschatology at all. There is however an assumption that the plural "YOU" audience (Ἀλλ᾽ ὑμῖν λέγω) can expect to be cursed, slapped, and dispossessed, there is an assumption of economic embeddedness, there is an assumption that some will have the ability to give and lend resources, and there is admonition against judging, and condemning. None of this follows neatly from an eschatological reversal based on class. One can of course, come up with different frameworks in which it can be made to follow; but if we are willing to do that, why not include the fourth blessing in the mix and see if the flow works better.

The best way to link the three blessings, which present an eschatological reversal, with the ethical injunctions of the rest of the Sermon is to introduce a covenantal aspect to the eschatology. This is not at all ad hoc, we see this move being made in the Hebrew Bible, Qumran documents such as the Damascus Document, as well as in the Psalms of Solomon and other Second Temple Jewish Literature. The idea is that the eschatological reversal happens through a covenantal group, a community, or a movement, but is ultimately realized by God. Within that framework, the blessings and the ethics fit together perfectly. Given this, there is much less reason to put the fourth blessing under a later redaction. The fourth blessing simply shifts the blessings from the eschatological classes (the destitute and the rich) to the covenantal community, who are on the side of the eschatological reversal (the "Son of Man" figure is almost always associated with an eschatological shift).[25]

Why though, must we accept that the blessings (and woes) must be originally tied to the rest of the Sermon? Dale Allison (along with others) has proposed that the blessings circulated separately from the rest of the Sermon. Dale Allison argues:

> The blessings at the beginning of the discourse (6:20–23), with their allusions to Isaiah 61, their mention of the "poor," and their implicit Christology, prepare for Jesus' answer to John the Baptists query about the coming one in Q7:18–23, which also alludes to Isaiah 61, refers to the poor and implicitly addresses Jesus' Identity.[26]

25. Betz, *A commentary on the Sermon on the Mount, including the Sermon on the Plain,* 572.

26. Allison, *Constructing Jesus,* 312n17.

Here Allison is basically arguing that Luke 7:18–23 portrays Jesus as "the coming one," a Christological title, and is thus likely a later redaction,[27] and that the blessings foreshadow Luke 7:18–23 and therefore they are also likely a later redaction. Whatever one thinks of the origin of Luke 7:18–23, there is no direct quotation of Isaiah 61—as there is in Luke 7:18–23—nor is there any direct reference to Isaiah 61, other than the use of the term "πτωχοί" in the blessings.[28] There likely is, however, an allusion to or memory of Isaiah 61 (as we will see below); however, the allusion is used in a completely different way than the way Luke 7:18–23 uses the direct quotation of Isaiah 61. The blessings' and woes' allusion to Isaiah 61 is used to speak of the eschatological fulfillment of that passage—which was a very common use of that passage at the time[29]—not any connection to Jesus himself. If Luke 7:18–23 is in fact post-Easter tradition, then it is likely that it draws on actual references to pre-Easter allusions to Isaiah 61 in the Jesus tradition. Rather, as stated earlier, a better reading of the blessings and woes is to read them as programmatic to the rest of the Sermon, providing the eschatological logic for the ethical commandments that follow. Another option for the origins of the blessings has been put forward by Douglas E Oakman:[30] the Aramaic introduction to the Passover *Haggadah*:

> This is the bread of poverty which our forefathers ate in the land of Egypt. Let all who are hungry enter and eat; let all who are needy come to our Passover feast. This year we are here; next year may we be in the Land of Israel. This year we are slaves; next year may we be free men. (*The Passover Haggadah* [Glatzer])

This parallel may very well be the context in which the blessings were to be understood. This would bring to mind the liberation of the Israelites from Egypt, which was a reversal of fortunes for all of Israel, from slavery and oppression to liberation and the promised land. This reversal of fortunes was (in the biblical tradition) the background of the Torah regulations; likewise, the reversal of the Sermon's blessings and woes is the background from which one is to understand the ethical commandments of the Sermon.

---

27. Both Burton Mack and John Kloppenborg agree with Allison with regards Luke 7:18–24. Mack, *The Lost Gospel*, 132; Kloppenborg, *The formation of Q*, 107–108.

28. Isaiah 61:2–3 shares the word πενθέω with the woes, however the woes use the term as something which will befall the ones laughing; whereas Isaiah promises comfort to the πενθοῦντας.

29. We will see examples of this later on in material from the Dead Sea Scrolls.

30. Oakman, *Jesus and the Peasants*, 104.

By themselves, the first three blessings and woes work as a kind of limerick, an easily remembered and rhythmic pattern bringing to mind the eschatological reversal. The fourth blessing and woe shifts the focus from the abstract, future *eschaton*, to the individual in community—breaking from the rhythmic pattern in order to address the person who aligns himself with the message of the first three blessings and woes (personified in the apocalyptic "Son of Man" figure). It then reminds the listener that being on the side of the eschatological reversal will put one on the margins of society, but that ultimately this is a good thing, since the prophets who are now revered were also marginalized. Then the Sermon continues addressing the person aligning himself with the message, providing the ethical instructions for how one being on the side of the message should live. The closest modern analogy I can think of that parallels this kind of thought is the Leninist idea of the proletarian revolution; in which the proletariat take power from the bourgeoisie (the eschatological reversal), but which is spearheaded by a revolutionary party that aligns itself with the proletariat class (the ones who are aligned with the "Son of Man" figure).

Further evidence of the unity of the blessings (and woes) comes from parallel sources: The Gospel of Matthew, the Gospel of Thomas, Polycarp's letter to the Philippians, and Paul's first letter to the Corinthians. Matthew includes the fourth blessing along with the first three and others (Matthew 5:3–12). The Gospel of Thomas includes the first blessing and a form of the fourth blessing, placing them together (Gospel of Thomas 52, 68–69). The same is true of one of the earliest attestations we have of the blessings (outside of the New Testament) in Polycarp's letter to the Philippians; where the blessing of the destitute and the blessing for those persecuted are taken together.

What is interesting about Polycarp's attestation is that it does not directly match the text of Luke, or Matthew, and certainly not the theorized Q1 or Q2. Here is Polycarp's rendition of the blessings:

μακάριοι οἱ πτωχοὶ

καὶ οἱ διωκόμενοι ἕνεκεν δικαιοσύνης, ὅτι αὐτῶν ἐστὶν ἡ βασιλεία τοῦ θεοῦ.

Blessed are the destitute.

And those persecuted on account of righteousness, because theirs is the Kingdom of God. (Polycarp, *Philippians*, 2.3 [Holmes])

The first part matches the opening words of Luke's first blessing "Μακάριοι οἱ πτωχοί," the second part does not match Luke's fourth blessing at all. It does however, match one of Matthew's blessings in his rendition of the blessings, specifically the one that comes right before Matthew's rendition of Luke's fourth blessing:

> μακάριοι οἱ δεδιωγμένοι ἕνεκεν δικαιοσύνης, ὅτι αὐτῶν ἐστιν ἡ βασιλεία τῶν οὐρανῶν.
>
> Blessed are those persecuted on account of righteousness, because theirs is the Kingdom of Heaven. (Matt 5:10)

Which is followed by Matthew's rendition of Luke's fourth blessing:

> μακάριοί ἐστε ὅταν ὀνειδίσωσιν ὑμᾶς καὶ διώξωσιν καὶ εἴπωσιν πᾶν πονηρὸν καθ᾽ ὑμῶν [ψευδόμενοι] ἕνεκεν ἐμοῦ.
>
> Blessed are you when people revile you and persecute you and utter all kinds of evil against you [falsely] on my account. (Matt 5:11)

This tells us a few things. First of all, it tells us that Polycarp was not simply copying from Q, Luke, or Matthew, since his text does not match any of them; likely he was working with oral tradition or memory.[31] Another thing it tells us is that whatever tradition Polycarp was dealing with combined the class based blessing with the blessing for those who are persecuted independently of Luke, Q, or Matthew; and is thus not dependent on redactions of Q.

Another interesting parallel is in 1 Corinthians in which Paul writes:

> To the present hour we are hungry and thirsty, we are poorly clothed and beaten and homeless, and we grow weary from the work of our own hands. When reviled, we bless; when persecuted, we endure; when slandered, we speak kindly. We have become like the rubbish of the world, the dregs of all things, to this very day. (1 Cor 4:11–13)

31. Michael Holmes (Holmes, "Polycarp's Letter to the Philippians and the Writings that later formed the New Testament," in Gregory and Tuckett, *The Reception of the New Testament in the Apostolic Fathers*, 193–197) argues that we cannot know if Polycarp drew from any written material, and that if he did, we cannot know what they were. However, we can say that it seems very unlikely indeed that Polycarp would have had two physical gospels (Matthew and Luke) in front of him. Another option is that Polycarp was using a form of Q which had Matthew's blessing on those persecuted for righteousness sake, which would require a Q reconstruction that differs from both Kloppenborg's and Mack's. Given the data we have, the best solution is that he is drawing from a source independent from Q, Luke, and Matthew; if I were to guess, an oral source.

Along with the preceding verse 8:

> Already (ἤδη) you have all you want! Already (ἤδη) you have become rich! Quite apart from us you have become kings! Indeed, I wish that you had become kings, so that we might be kings with you! (1 Cor 4:8)

Here we have a class-based reversal: even though we are hungry, thirsty, poorly clothed, homeless, and so on, we are actually kings. Interestingly, Paul uses the term "Already" (ἤδη), this echoes the use of the present tense in the first blessing where it says the Kingdom of God is YOURS (ὑμετέρα ἐστὶν). It is very likely that Paul knows a very early version of the Sermon,[32] but the very different wording and structure of 1 Corinthians 4:8–13 compared to the Sermon hints that there is no literary dependence. However, like Matthew, Polycarp, and Thomas, Paul combines the idea of socio-economic reversal with the idea that Jesus's followers are persecuted (in verses 12–13).

The examples give us evidence of very early renderings or allusions to a blessing of the destitute that is combined with an idea of the persecuted righteous.

What about the woes? Despite many "Q" theorists' opinions that the woes are a Lukan invention; there is in my estimation good reasons for considering them pre-Lukan. For example, there are parallels in James, such as:

> ταλαιπωρήσατε καὶ πενθήσατε καὶ κλαύσατε· ὁ γέλως ὑμῶν εἰς πένθος μετατραπήτω καὶ ἡ χαρὰ εἰς κατήφειαν·
>
> Lament and mourn and weep. Let your laughter be turned into mourning and your joy into dejection. (Jas 4:9)

This verse, especially the reversal from laughing (γέλως) to mourning (πένθος), and the combination of mourning and weeping (πενθήσατε καὶ κλαύσατε), links to the woes in Luke 6:25. Also, a later passage in James:

> Ἄγε νῦν οἱ πλούσιοι, κλαύσατε ὀλολύζοντες ἐπὶ ταῖς ταλαιπωρίαις ὑμῶν ταῖς ἐπερχομέναις.
>
> Come now, you rich people, weep and wail for the miseries that are coming to you. (Jas 5:1)

---

32. Allison, *Constructing Jesus*, 313–314; Robinson, "Kerygma and History in the New Testament," in Robinson and Koester, *Trajectories through Early Christianity*, 43–46.

links with Luke 6:24 in that it envisions a class-based reversal: a calamity for the rich. This points to an early tradition of eschatological reversal, not just focused on blessings for the disadvantaged, but also on calamity for the privileged. These two parallels in James also raise the possibility that the author of James knew the woes independently of Luke, which would require them to not be a Lukan creation. Another clue that the woes might not be a Lukan invention is that the term woe (οὐαί) appears in five pericopes in Luke outside of the Sermon on the Plain (Luke 10:13; 11:42–52; 17:1; 21:23; 22:22); the first three are part of the "Q" material,[33] 21:23 is material shared with both Mark and Matthew, and 22:22 is also shared with both Mark and Matthew but both Matthew and Luke adds the "woe" to the Markan material, none are purely Lukan inventions. The parallelism that the woes have with the blessings make it unlikely that they circulated separately prior to the writing of Luke's gospel; which leaves us with the probability that they are original to Luke's source. For these reasons it is reasonable to believe that the woes are pre-Lukan.

When it comes to the blessings and woes, the best way of reading them is as a block, starting with the contrast between the destitute class/rich class and the eschatological shift, then moving on to the fourth blessing and woe which addresses the audience of disciples who desire to be allied with the Kingdom of God; and gives a sobering reminder that those on the side of the Kingdom of God are not going to be spoken well of in the present age. Reading the blessings and woes as a block allows us to treat the blessings and woes as many scholars have (for good reason) wanted to treat them: as programmatic.[34]

Let us now take a look at the socio-economic nature of the blessings and woes. Some have suggested that the blessings and woes should not be thought of socio-economically; but rather spiritually. One commentator who suggested this is Charles H. Talbert in his commentary *Reading Luke: A Literary and Theological Commentary on the Third Gospel*. His argument begins with the claim that the gospel canonizes no sociological state.[35] There are a few things to say about that: first, if we are taking the Sermon on the Plain to be mostly going back to Jesus (which I believe we have good reason for doing), or a pre-Lukan source, then we can isolate Jesus's sayings

---

33. According to the reconstructions of Burton Mack and John Kloppenborg. Mack, *The Lost Gospel*, 81–102; Kloppenborg, *Q: The Earliest Gospel*, 123–144.

34. Tuckett, *Q and the History of Early Christianity*, 427–428.

35. Talbert, *Reading Luke*, 73.

from the gospels—which have their own theological purposes in their presentations—and see if he (or it) does in fact canonize a socio-economic
state; in short, the fact that Luke does not canonize something does not
exclude the possibility that Jesus (or the pre-Lukan source) did. Second, we
actually can say that Luke in fact does—if not canonize poverty—at least
place the destitute as a group on the side of the Kingdom of God in contexts
where the term "destitute" (or similar phrases) has clear socio-economic
connotations.[36]

His other argument is that within the Hebrew bible and second temple
Jewish literature there are examples of sociological terms being used of
groups which defined the groups not sociologically, but rather spiritually
or morally. When it comes to "the poor"[37] he uses a few examples. One
is the term עָנִי found in Isaiah 61:1, which he renders as "meek," in the
Masoretic text, but which is translated (πτωχοῖς) "poor" (or destitute) in
the LXX;[38] this argument can simply be left aside by pointing out that the
original word in the Masoretic text can also mean "oppressed"[39]—which
certainly has socio-economic connotations. However, the fact that the LXX
translates "meek" (or oppressed, עָנִי) into "poor" (πτωχοῖς) should lead to
the obvious conclusion that the LXX translators viewed the "poor" as being
meek (or oppressed), not that the "poor" were to be redefined as anyone
who happens to have the quality of meekness (or anyone who happens to
be under some kind of oppression).

He also points out that in some ancient Jewish documents, such
as some of the Qumran documents, the poor are described as counting
worldly goods as nothing; the devout and the poor are linked to the pious.[40] The problem with using these connections of "the poor" and certain
attributes to redefine "the poor" as nothing more than those attributes is
that by doing so Talbert is, in a sense, putting the cart before the horse.
The fact that attributes are linked with a socio-economic class only implies
that this socio-economic class is associated with these attributes, not that

36. For example: Luke 1:46–55; 4:18–19; 7:22; 14:13–14; 16:19–31; 18:22.

37. I will translate πτωχος as "poor" rather than "destitute" when considering Charles
H. Talbert's theory since that is the translation that he uses.

38. Talbert, *Reading Luke*, 73.

39. The Brown-Driver-Briggs Lexicon has Isaiah 61:1's use of the term עָנִי defined as
"*poor and weak*, oppressed by rich and powerful," rather than "poor, afflicted, humble,
meek." The HALOT Lexicon has the term defined as "bowed" which can have the connotation of meekness, but also of being dejected.

40. Talbert, *Reading Luke*, 73–74.

the socio-economic class has been redefined as those attributes; in other words, it is the class possessing the attributes, not the attributes possessing the class. Let us take as an example the statement "rich people are greedy" and then a later pronounced statement of "I do not like rich people." The fact that rich people are associated with greed does not mean that the second statement can be redefined as "I do not like greedy people." What a proper exegesis would say is that what the two statements taken together mean is that the individual does not like rich people because he believes rich people to be greedy (or simply that he does not like rich people for whatever reason, and he also believes them to be greedy). The direct object of his dislike is the socio-economic class of "rich people," not the abstract notion of "greed." If you press the individual further, it may be that, deep down, he actually only has a problem with greed, not the socio-economic class; and he only dislikes "the rich" because he believes them to be greedy. It may also be the case that he does not like the rich as a socio-economic class for various reasons, one of which may be that they are greedy. Either way, it is not the job of an exegete to psycho-analyze a writer, it is the job of an exegete to find out what the writer is conveying in his text. This argument shows that the writers of the LXX or the Qumran documents are not necessarily defining "the poor" as the attributes they assign to "the poor." But even if they were, that in no way warrants reading Luke's usage of "the poor" in the blessing to mean some attribute, unless there is some qualification demanding that reading in the text itself. Yet the only qualification we get is that "the poor" are contrasted with "the rich" and listed along with "hunger" and "weeping."

For the other blessings and woes Talbert also has arguments for reading them as spiritual rather than sociological. For example, he points out that "the Rich" are described in 1 Enoch as those who trust in their riches, and that in Luke 12:16–21; 16:19–25[41] they are described as ignoring God and neighbor.[42] The same problem with Talbert's argument spiritualizing the poor applies to his spiritualizing the rich: the fact that attributes are assigned to a socio-economic group does not warrant redefining that socio-economic group as the attributes assigned to it.

For Talbert's reading to work we need everything to be spiritualized: for "the poor" to mean "those who depend on God" (or some other spiritualized meaning) and "the rich" must mean "those who do not depend on

---

41. Both of these passages are only found in Luke.

42. Talbert, *Reading Luke*, 74.

God" rather than "the rich," and "the hungry" must mean those "spiritually hungry" rather than people who need to eat, and so on and so forth. At this point Talbert would just be reading into the text what is not there. The fact that Matthew qualifies things like "poor" with "in spirit," and "hunger" with "for righteousness" is evidence that we should take Luke's blessings and woes literally. If Matthew—who was writing to a Jewish audience that would presumably be much more familiar with the spiritual use of socio-economic terms compared to Luke's audience—included things like "τῷ πνεύματι" and "τὴν δικαιοσύνην" to qualify his socio-economic terms as having a spiritual application; then one would conclude that it would behoove Luke to also include those qualifications even more so, given that his audience would be less familiar with the spiritual use of socio-economic terms. However, in the Sermon on the Plain no such qualification exists, either for the blessings or the woes.

The blessings and woes in the Sermon on the Plain have the function of setting up the overarching worldview that will inform the rest of the Sermon. We start with an apocalyptic view: the *cosmos* has an eschatological *telos* which is one of social reversal—and then we go on to how one is to organize one's life and community in light of that in the rest of the Sermon.

Poverty, Wealth, and Reversal in Second Temple Judaism

The blessings and woes of Luke 6:20–26 reflect an eschatological *kerygma* of reversal: the reversal is instantiated in the here and now in the blessing of the poor and the woe to the rich, and effects of this reversal are guaranteed in the future. The blessings and woes also reflect the idea that the powers that be, the larger society, is against this reversal; and that those who are for it can expect to be ostracized. This style of teaching was part of the milieu of Second Temple Judaism, there were people who supported this kind of idea, and those who opposed it. Jesus's reversal teaching was part of a conversation that was already going on within the Jewish culture of the time.

Jesus's most common interlockers in the gospels are the Pharisees, whose teachings are partially recorded in the Mishnah.[43] Among the rulings regarding marriage, Rabbi Meir says the following:

---

43. This conclusion, although traditionally accepted, has been challenged, especially by Jacob Neusner (for example in his book *Judaism: The Evidence of the Mishnah*). However, the majority of scholarship on this issue still maintains a connection between the earliest stratum of the Mishnah and the Pharisees of the second temple period. For an

> A man should always teach his son a cleanly craft, and let him pray to him to whom riches and possessions belong, for there is no craft wherein there is not both poverty and wealth; for poverty comes not from a man's craft, nor riches from a man's craft, but all is according to merit. (Mishnah, *Kiddushin*. 4.14 [Danby])

The point here is that one should teach his son a clean craft—and stay away from the less honorable professions—however, at the very end we get a piece of familiar wisdom: wealth depends on merit. Rabbi Jonathan takes a similar point tying wealth and poverty with fulfilling or neglecting the Torah:

> R. Jonathan said: He that fulfills the Law in poverty shall in the end fulfill it in wealth; and he that neglects the Law in wealth shall in the end neglect it in poverty. (Mishnah, *Aboth*. 4.9)

This fits with the general view of the Rabbi's with regards to wealth and poverty: wealth comes not only from hard work or business savvy; but also, from righteousness and merit. This view of wealth and poverty spilled over to legal rulings. For example, the damages given to someone who was injured partially depended on the social status, the class, of the one who inflicts damage and the one who suffers damage. In the Mishnah, there are five different levels of liability when it comes to injury: the injury itself, the pain suffered, healing, time lost, and indignity inflicted. In explaining the liability of indignity, the ruling of the Sages is:

> For 'indignity inflicted'—all is in accordance with [the condition of life of] him that inflicts and him that suffers the indignity. (Mishnah, *Baba Kamma*. 8.1)

The condition of life will raise or lower the "indignity inflicted." In theory, a beggar on the street who strikes a prince will be more liable than the prince who strikes the beggar on the street, since the loss of dignity is greater for someone with a higher "condition of life" than it is for someone of a lower "condition of life." This legal ruling attaches human dignity with social status, even in the court of law.[44] If we think of Rabbi Jonathan and Rabbi

---

extended discussion of the connection between the Mishnah and the Pharisees of the second temple period. See Sanders, *Jewish Law from Jesus to the Mishnah*, 131–254.

44. This ruling is debated over in the Talmud, with Rabbi Meir arguing that all Jews are of equal value, since they are all sons of Abraham, Isaac, and Jacob; and Rabbi Yehuda arguing that the stature of a person should determine how the court views him or her; and then there is Rabbi Shimon who agrees with Rabbi Yehuda but goes on to argue that the rich person should be considered a freeman who lost his property and that a poor

Meir's principles that we talked about above; this legal ruling, with its concomitant principle, follows logically. If it is the case that riches and poverty are the result of real merit (generally speaking), it follows that the rich and the poor are themselves of different merit, different value.

If an individual is poor, according to this logic, it is because he lacks righteousness, he lacks worth, thus he is of less worth; it is just that he is poor, and it is just that he lacks dignity. If an individual is rich it is because he is righteous, he is worthy, and if he suffers indignity it is an injustice. Thus, if a poor person is treated in an undignified manner, no great injustice has been done, that poor person is already of less worth; yet if a rich person is treated in an undignified manner, this is a problem—he deserves better.

A popular genre in the second temple period was wisdom literature. Following parts of the Psalms and books like Proverbs, second temple wisdom literature consisted of statements, stories, and allegories intended to impart wisdom and teachings about virtue to the audience. Some second temple wisdom literature fits with the idea of a reversal of wealth, tying wealth with injustice, and the poor with the oppressed—for example, in Sirach we find some surprisingly outspoken analyses of class conflict:

> Do not lift a weight too heavy for you, or associate with one stronger and richer than you. How will the clay pot associate with the cauldron? The former will strike against, and the former will be smashed. A rich person (πλούσιος) did wrong, and he was angry to boot; a poor person (πτωχὸς) has been wronged, and he will plead. If you are useful, he will work with you, and if you are in want, he will abandon you. If you have something, he will live with you; and he will clean you out, and he will not suffer. He has need of you and will deceive you and will smile at you and give you hope; he will speak nice things to you and say, "What do you need?" He will shame you with his food, until he cleans you out two or three times, and at last he will mock you; after these things, he will see you and leave you and will shake his head at you. (Sirach 13:2–7 [NETS])
>
> . . .
>
> Every living thing loves what is like to it, and every person his fellow. All flesh congregates according to kind, and with one like himself will a man cleave. What will a wolf have in common with a lamb?—so is a sinner to a pious person. What peace is there

---

person should be considered least among the poor, so as to lessen the compensation owed by the perpetrator. (Babylonian Talmud, *Baba Kamma*. 86a.)

between a hyena and a dog? And what peace between a rich person (πλουσίῳ) and a needy person? The prey of lions is onagers in the desert; thus the poor (πτωχοί) are the fodder of the rich (πλουσίων). An abomination to a proud person is humility; thus an abomination to a rich person (πλουσίῳ) is a poor person (πτωχός).

When a rich person totters, he is supported by friends, but when a humble falls, he is pushed away by friends. When a rich person staggers, many are his helpers; he spoke things not to be spoken, and they justified him. A humble person staggered, and in addition they rebuked him; he uttered sense, and no place was given to him. A rich person spoke, and they all kept silent, and they exalted his words to the clouds. A poor person spoke, and they said, "Who is this?" And if he should stumble, they will even overturn him. Wealth in which there is no sin is good, but in the mouths of an impious person poverty is wicked. (Sirach 13:15–25)

This kind of class politics might make even a doctrinaire Marxist blush—nevertheless, it does fit with the worldview present in the blessings and woes of the Sermon on the Plain. The terms for "rich" and "poor" are the same terms that Luke uses in the blessings and woes (πλούσιος and πτωχός), indicating that we are speaking about the same kinds of class categories. In this text, Sirach claims that the rich will always exploit and oppress the poor, and that the poor are the victims of this oppression—leading to the conclusion that there cannot be any peace between the rich and the poor. The rich are spoken of as proud, deceitful, cruel, and selfish.

If this was a common view in second temple Judaism, one could see how an eschatological ideology, an ideology of restoration, would include a class reversal. The wealth of the rich comes from injustice and exploitation, and the poor (who are also called the humble) are the victims; so for justice to be restored, a reversal would have to take place. However, we see near the end a slight qualification: "Wealth in which there is no sin is good." This seems like a strange departure from the strong language that precedes it; however, it makes sense given other discussions of wealth and poverty in Sirach that seem to defend wealth, and actually go against the idea of a class reversal:

Happy is a rich person (πλούσιος) who was found blameless, and who did not go after gold. Who is he and shall we call him happy? For he did wonders among his people. Who has been tested by it and been made perfect? And it will be as a boast for him. Who was able to transgress and did not transgress, and to do evil and did not do so? Therefore his good things will be confirmed, and his acts of charity an assembly will recount [ἐλεημοσύνας, can also be translated as almsgiving[45]]. (Sirach 31:8–11)

. . .

Gold and silver make a foot firm, and above both counsel is highly esteemed. Money and strength will lift up a heart, and above both is fear of the Lord; there is no want in the fear of the Lord, and with it there is no reason to seek aid. Fear of the Lord is like an orchard of blessing, and more than any glory it covers him. (Sirach 40:25–27)

The first passage speaks of the good rich person, who uses his wealth in a good way: giving alms, doing good things, not succumbing to the temptation to transgress, and so on. In the second passage it speaks of wealth as a good thing in a practical sense, but less good than fear of the Lord. These tendencies seem to moderate Sirach's view of class: yes, the rich are oppressors, but not all of them, and the rich do have the opportunity to be righteous if they use their riches correctly. In Sirach 11 we get full agreement with the ideology of the Mishnaic Rabbis:

Good things and bad, life and death, poverty and wealth are from the Lord . . . The Lord's gift remains with the pious, and his favor will bring success forever. (Sirach 11:14, 17)

This passage is in complete concert with the idea that wealth comes from merit; in fact, it comes from the Lord himself—the wealthy are rich because God rewarded them. Continuing we read this:

There exists one who will become rich from his diligence and miserliness, and this is the portion of his recompense. When he says, "I have found rest, and now I will eat of my good things," even he does not know how time will pass by, and he will leave them to others and will die. Stand by your covenant, and attend to it and, in your work grow old. Do not wonder at the works of a sinner, but have faith in the Lord, and continue your labor, because it is easy in the eyes of the Lord quickly, suddenly, to make a needy person rich. The Lord's blessing is in the wage of a pious person, and in a short time his good pleasure flourishes. (Sirach 11:18–22)

The poor can receive God's blessing as well, and become rich, if they work hard and become diligent in their work. This view seems to go contrary to the class warfare narrative of Sirach 13. In these passages, wealth and poverty are the result of God's blessing and dependent on one's righteousness,

45. BDAG, ἐλεημοσύνη.

this supports the merit view of wealth and also the view that the poor, in general, are basically poor due to their own failings. This is just one example of wisdom literature, but the pattern is found elsewhere in other wisdom literature.[46]

As we have seen in Sirach—and as one can read in other wisdom literature—the wisdom literature presents us with a mixed bag: on the one hand wealth and poverty are the just deserts of diligence, hard work, and merit; on the other hand, it is recognized that exploitation and oppression are real forces and that these forces explain class distinctions. In much of this literature, class warfare is as real as hard work and God's blessings.

Other tendencies within second temple Judaism agreed strongly with the idea of class conflict and fully supported the idea of a class-based reversal. One very popular work in second temple Judaism was the apocalyptic Book of Enoch. In chapters 94 to 100, the work lists certain woes on sinners, oppressors, the unrighteous, and so on; part of the group receiving woes are the rich:

> Woe unto you, O rich people! For you have put your trust in your wealth. You shall ooze out of your riches, for you do not remember the Most High. (1 Enoch 94:8 [Isaac])
>
> . . .
>
> Woe unto you, you sinners! For your money makes you appear like the righteous, but your hearts do reprimand you like real sinners, this very matter shall be a witness against you, as a record of your evil deeds.
>
> Woe unto you who eat the best bread. And drink wine in large bowls, trampling upon the weak people with your might. (1 Enoch 96:4–5)
>
> . . .
>
> Woe unto you who gain silver and gold by unjust means; you will then say, 'We have grown rich and accumulated goods, we have acquired everything that we have desired. So now let us do whatever we like; for we have gathered silver, we have filled our treasuries (with money) like water.
>
> And many are the laborers in our houses.' Your lies flow like water. For your wealth shall not endure but it shall take off from you quickly for you have acquired it all unjustly, and you shall be given over to a great curse. (1 Enoch 97:8–10)

---

46. For example compare Proverbs 10:4, 22; 12:27; 22:16 with Proverbs 13:23; 14:31; 22:7.

Like much apocalyptic Jewish literature, 1 Enoch equates the rich with the unrighteous and places them under God's judgement. The author of 1 Enoch does not talk about the rich who are sinners, or the sinners who are rich; rather, the sinners are the rich and the rich are the sinners. These rich sinners, however, are due to receive God's judgement; in fact, 1 Enoch says that these rich sinners will be killed by the righteous with God's blessing (1 *Enoch* 91:11). In speaking about the general attitude towards the relationship between socio-economic class and the identity of "sinners," James Crossley says:

> Whenever the socioeconomic status of sinners is mentioned in Jewish sources it is perfectly clear who they were and who they were not: they were not to be associated primarily with the poor, the exploited, the uneducated, or the ordinary folk but rather the better off, the exploiters, and the lawless rich—people, in other words, who might as well have been Gentile oppressors.[47]

This sentiment agrees with the sentiment found in the blessings and woes of the Sermon on the Plain; the *eschaton* is class based, and the rich are under judgement.

We also find this sentiment in apocalyptic literature found among the Qumran documents, for example the Messianic Apocalypse (4Q521):

> For the Lord will consider the pious (Hasidim) and call the righteous by name.
>
> Over the poor His spirit will hover and will renew the faithful with His power.
>
> And He will glorify the pious on the throne of the eternal Kingdom.
>
> . . .
>
> For He will heal the wounded, and revive the dead and bring good news to the poor (Isa lxi, 1).
>
> . . . He will lead the uprooted and make the hungry rich . . . (4Q521 2 [Vermes])

Here we have a direct reference to an eschatological reversal: the hungry will be rich and the good news is good news for the poor. One thing to note here is that Isaiah 61 is referenced, Isaiah 61 is also referenced by Jesus in his mission statement in the synagogue of Nazareth, and within Isaiah 61 the Jubilee is explicitly referenced: the redistribution of land and the releasing of debt slaves—the reversal. The apocalyptic "War Scroll" (1QM, 1Q33,

47. Crossley, *Why Christianity Happened*, 95.

4Q491 7, 4Q471) describes the final battle between the "Sons of Light" and the "Sons of Darkness," the language of the poor being redeemed and being the beneficiaries of a reversal is also found there:

> by the hand of Thy poor whom Thou hast redeemed [by Thy might] and by the fullness of Thy marvelous power. (Thou hast opened) the door of hope to the melting heart: Thou wilt do to them as Thou didst to Pharaoh, and to the captains of his chariots in the Red Sea. Thou wilt kindle the downcast of spirit and they shall be a flaming torch in the straw to consume ungodliness and never to cease till iniquity is destroyed.
>
> . . .
>
> For Thou wilt deliver into the hands of the poor the enemies from all the lands, to humble the mighty of the peoples by the hand of those bent to the dust, to bring upon the [head of Thine enemies] the reward of the wicked, and to justify Thy true judgement in the midst of all the sons of men, and to make for Thyself an everlasting Name among the people [whom Thou hast redeemed] (1QM 11)

The poor, those bent to the dust, the downcast of spirit, will be the redeemed; and the enemies and the wicked will be handed over to them. In this case the "enemies" are the Kittim (perhaps the Greeks, perhaps the Romans), an earthy military power dominating the "poor" of God. These enemies are also thought to be under the power of Belial; the enemies are an earthly military, and the redeemed are the downcast poor, but the fight is ultimately between heavenly forces. The Kittim are on the side of Belial, and the poor are on the side of God, but the poor of God will be victorious.

Another clear example of a reversal—specifically the economic reversal of the Jubilee—being tied with eschatology in the Qumran documents is in the Heavenly Prince Melchizedek document:

> And concerning that which He said, In [this] year of Jubilee [each of you shall return to his property (Lev xxv, 13); and likewise, And this is the manner of release:] every creditor shall release that which he has lent [to his neighbour. He shall not exact it of his neighbour and his brother], for God's release [has been proclaimed] (Deut xv, 2). [And it will be proclaimed at] the end of days concerning the captives as [He said, To proclaim liberty to the captives (Isa lxi, 1). Its interpretation is that He] will assign them to the Sons of Heaven and to the inheritance of Melchizedek; f[or He will cast] their [lot] amid the po[rtions of Melchize]dek, who will return

> them there and will proclaim to them liberty, forgiving them [the
> wrong-doings] of all their iniquities. (11Q13 2)

Here we see the Jubilee (along with the Sabbatical law)—which is explicitly
an economic reversal: a redistribution of land, a releasing of debts, and a
releasing of debt slaves—interpreted eschatologically. The "Sons of Heaven"
will have their wrong-doings forgiven so that they can take their positions
as Melchizedek-style kings and priests. Later on, this eschatological vision
is explained further:

> And
>
> Melchizedek will avenge the vengeance of the judgements of God . . .
> and he will drag [them from the hand of] Belial and from the hand of all
> the sp[irits of] his [lot]. And all the 'gods [of Justice'] will come to his aid
> [to] attend to the de[struction] of Belial. And the height is . . . all the sons
> of God . . . this . . . This is the day of [Peace/Salvation] concerning which
> [God] spoke [through Isa]iah the prophet. (11Q13 2)

Here we see the reversal, the cosmic reversal. Belial is overthrown, and
"Melchizedek" is aided by the gods (this is a reference to the gods in YH-
WH's council in Psalms 82) of justice. The result of this overthrow of Belial
is the day of Peace and Salvation. The economic reversal of the Jubilee and
Sabbatical year—meant to secure social equality and social justice—is interpreted cosmically by the Heavenly Melchizedek document to refer to a
cosmic reversal securing cosmic peace, salvation, and justice.

The Qumran documents include many sentiments of God protecting
the poor and siding with the poor; but these, along with some others,[48] go
a step further, speaking of an economic and social reversal, which is ultimately based on a cosmic reversal: the victory of God over the wicked spirit
powers on behalf of the poor and against the powerful.

Another document I want to look at is the Psalms of Solomon, written in the first century BCE.[49] The Psalms of Solomon describe wealthy

---

48. For example: For He humbles the proud spirit with no remnant and from the dust
He lifts up the poor to [eternal heights]. (4Q427 2); And: Interpreted, this concerns the
congregation of the Poor, who [shall possess] the whole world as an inheritance. They
shall possess the High Mountain of Israel [for ever], and shall enjoy [everlasting] delights
in His Sanctuary. [But those who] shall be cut off, they are the violent [of the nations and]
the wicked of Israel; they shall be cut off and blotted out for ever. (4Q171 3)

49. Charlesworth, *The Apocrypha and Pseudepigrapha of the Old Testament in English*, 629–630.

and powerful "sinners" who had become insolent in their prosperity.[50] The "sinners" are to be punished, and their punishment will be forever;[51] the sinners are separated from the righteous, who are to be saved and shown pity.[52] Part of the faith of the author of the Psalms of Solomon comes from his conviction that his God is the one who favors the poor:

> O Lord God, I will praise your name with joy in the midst of those who have knowledge of your righteous judgments. For you are kind and merciful, the refuge of the poor (πτωχοῦ); when I cry out to you, do not pass me by in silence. (Psalms of Solomon 5:1–2 [NETS])
>
> . . .
>
> You feed kings and rulers and peoples, O God, and who is the hope of the poor and needy (πτωχοῦ καὶ πένητος), unless it be you O Lord? (Psalms of Solomon 5:11)
>
> . . .
>
> And the devout shall acknowledge in the assembly of the people, and God will show pity upon the poor (πτωχοὺς) to the joy of Israel. (Psalms of Solomon 10:6)

These three passages show that the assurance that the author of the Psalms of Solomon has that God will save the righteous is based on his conviction that God loves the poor (better translated the destitute). Even if at the present time the sinners are in power and are wealthy; the writer of the Psalms of Solomon can take comfort in the hope that the situation will be reversed, because God punishes the proud, and shows pity on the destitute. One can understand why—given the near constant domination of Israel by foreign powers much wealthier than Israel—this kind of literature would be popular.

After a quick survey of these three genres of Jewish writings (rabbinic, wisdom, and apocalyptic), we see a plethora of different views of wealth and poverty and class dynamics. However, we see in Jesus—in the blessings and woes of the Sermon on the Plain—a rejection of the general Pharisaic school of thought (and some strands of the wisdom tradition), and an endorsement of the apocalyptic view (and some other strands of the wisdom tradition). Jesus's introduction to the Sermon on the Plain fits perfectly with an apocalyptic genre and worldview; and it would have been understood

---

50. Psalms of Solomon 1:4–6.

51. For example, Psalms of Solomon 2:16–17; 3:11–12; 13:11; 14:9; 15:5–12.

52. For example, Psalms of Solomon 2:34–35; 3:12; 9:5–7; 10:3–4; 13:6, 11–12; 14:10.

by the original audience as such. This would not have necessarily sounded like the introduction to a sermon on ethics; but rather, the introduction to an eschatological vision of the destruction of the powers that be, and a glorification of the downtrodden.

Outside of the rabbinic, wisdom, and apocalyptic writings we have writings written by Jews to Gentiles (this would include the Luke-Acts work as well as other New Testament writings like the Gospel of John); one of the most famous examples of a Jewish writer writing to Gentiles is Josephus. In chapter 8 of book 4 of his History of the Jews Josephus explains the usury laws and the laws on taking collateral for loans, after explaining that if a poor person gives collateral for a loan the creditor must return it (especially if it is something like a garment) before sundown whether or not the loan has been repaid, he gives this explanatory line:

> God himself naturally showing mercy to the poor.
>
> φύσει τοῦ θεοῦτοῖς πενομένοις ἔλεον νέμοντος. (Josephus, A.J., 4.8.26)

Here Josephus is using a form of πένης which is more akin to the working-class poor and has less of a connotation of destitution as πτωχός. Nevertheless, in this proposition Josephus explains the basis for the lending laws: God, by nature, shows mercy to the poor. This idea cannot be taken for granted, the Greco-Roman gods were not always friendly to the poor; and Josephus himself betrays negative views of the poor in that they often joined up with the wicked in sedition.[53] In making this claim and connecting it to part of the Mosaic Law, Josephus is teaching his gentile readership about the God of Israel, about how the God of Israel is to be understood; in contrast to other gods.

Poverty, Wealth, and Reversal in the Hebrew Bible

Going further back we find a lot of writings touching on wealth, poverty, and class dynamics in the Hebrew Bible.

---

53. Josephus, A.J., 15.10.2 (the poorer soldiers were used by enemies of Herod, and were troublesome); Josephus, J.W., 2.17.6 (the poor were bought over to the rebels by the destruction of the debt records); Josephus, J.W., 4.6.3 (a positive outcome of zealots killing those who escaped the city was that the rich bought their way out and only the poor died); Josephus, J.W., 7.11.1 (the poor were the ones that listened to Jonathan the Sacarii).

Likely, the most important passage of the Hebrew Bible in relation to the blessings and woes is Isaiah 61:

> The spirit of the Lord God is upon me, because the Lord has anointed me; he has sent me to bring good news to the oppressed, to bind up the brokenhearted, to proclaim liberty to the captives, and release to the prisoners; to proclaim the year of the Lord's favor, and the day of vengeance of our God; to comfort all who mourn; (Isa 61:1–2 [NRSV])[54]

Along with Isaiah 58:

> Is not this the fast that I choose: to loose the bonds of injustice, to undo the thongs of the yoke, to let the oppressed go free, and to break every yoke? (Isa 58:6)

Isaiah 61:1–2 is quoted, borrowing a line from Isaiah 58:6, directly in the mission statement of Jesus given in his hometown synagogue (mentioned earlier, but which bears repeating), which reads:

> The Spirit of the Lord is upon me, because he has anointed me to bring good news to the poor.
> He has sent me to proclaim release to the captives and recovery of sight to the blind, to let the oppressed go free, to proclaim the year of the Lord's favor. (Luke 4:18–19)

Here Jesus is summing up what is to follow in his ministry, this is his mission statement.[55] In Luke 4:21 Jesus ties this passage to himself, claiming that it is fulfilled in him. The connection between the blessings and woes and Isaiah 61:1–2 is not as clear as the connection between Isaiah 61:1–2 and Luke 4:18–19, but I think it is there and can be demonstrated.

The closest direct connection comes from the Matthean version of the blessing about the mourners/weepers, that version renders it:

> "Blessed are those who mourn, for they will be comforted.
>
> μακάριοι οἱ πενθοῦντες, ὅτι αὐτοὶ παρακληθήσονται. (Matt 5:4)

In the LXX version of Isaiah 61:2 it says:

---

54. This section of the book—"Poverty, Wealth, and Reversal in the Hebrew Bible"—uses the NRSV translation of the Hebrew bible for quotation of the Hebrew Bible unless otherwise stated.

55. Talbert, *Reading Luke,* 60. Tuckett, *Q and the History of Early Christianity,* 227. Tuckett argues that Luke 4:16ff is actually part of the Q material, part of his argument is the prevalence of the theology of Isaiah 61 in Q.

To comfort all who mourn. [NETS]

παρακαλέσαι πάντας τοὺς πενθοῦντας.

Rather than πενθέω and παρακαλέω, Luke uses κλαίω and γελάω (although he does use πενθέω in the woes).[56] However all three—Matthew, Luke, and Isaiah—use πτωχοῖς. If the original sermon did allude to Isaiah 61 (as I believe is rather likely) it would fit with the eschatological and prophetic message of Jesus. The "poor" and "oppressed" in the Hebrew bible are the ones whom God cares about; and because of this, Israel has an obligation to care for them as well.[57] This pattern explains why Isaiah 61 goes directly from God giving good news to the poor to giving good news to Israel as a whole.[58] Going back to the blessings and woes with this in mind, we can understand the first three blessings—to the underclass in the age to come—as simply a continuation of the belief that God is on the side of the underclass; and we can understand the fourth blessing as a promise that those who fulfill their obligation to the poor (those who are on the side of the eschatological "Son of man") will also receive blessings. This is basic Jewish covenantal theology, God's concerns are to be his people's concerns, and blessings will follow; but if his concerns are ignored, calamity will follow.[59]

Thus, we have a connection between the blessings and woes, Jesus's mission statement in Luke 4:18–19, and Isaiah 58 and 61, with the common thread of the Jubilee running through all of them. The "Good year of the Lord" in Isaiah 61 is a direct reference to the Jubilee year.[60] But Isaiah 58 and 61 are connected to each other as well with regards to the Jubilee concept—Darrell Bock puts it this way:

> Isaiah 58 contains a prophetic rebuke of the nation for not exhibiting justice toward those in their nation who are in need. There God declares that the fast he prefers is one that treats one's neighbor properly. Isaiah 61 proclaims a time like that envisioned but not carried out by the nation in Isaiah 58. The two passages belong together because the release pictured in Isaiah 58 has Jubilee

---

56. Tuckett, *Q and the History of Early Christianity*, 223–224.

57. For example: Exodus 22:25–27; 23:10–11; Leviticus 19:9–10; Deuteronomy 15:7–11; 2 Samuel 22:28; Psalms 35:10; 72:2, 4, 12; Isaiah 26:6; 49:13.

58. Compare Isaiah 61 to Isaiah 62; 61 is about the socio-economic underclass, whereas 62 is about Israel as a whole.

59. Tuckett, *Q and the History of Early Christianity*, 428.

60. Bock, *The Theology of Luke and Acts*, 136.

overtones and also describes release in Sabbath terms, an event much like the year of Jubilee.[61]

The narrative laid out starting in Isaiah 58 has God's disappointment at Israel's lack of Justice for the poor—pictured in Sabbatical terms, the Sabbatical legislation being conceptually tied to the Jubilee legislation—followed by the declaration that justice will be fulfilled by God himself. Elsewhere in Isaiah we encounter similar ideas, for example:

> Ah, you who make iniquitous decrees, who write oppressive statutes, to turn aside the needy from justice and to rob the poor of my people of their right, that widows may be your spoil, and that you may make the orphans your prey!
>
> What will you do on the day of punishment, in the calamity that will come from far away? To whom will you flee for help, and where will you leave your wealth, so as not to crouch among the prisoners or fall among the slain? For all this his anger has not turned away; his hand is stretched out still. (Isa 10:1–4)

Rather than God guaranteeing justice, here we see God guaranteeing punishment for the powerful purveyors of injustice. Although in the woes of the Sermon on the Plain's blessing and woes there is no direct indication that the loss of wealth and fortune of the rich is necessarily divine punishment for injustice—rather than simply the outcome of the Kingdom of God—the parallel of the reversal of fortunes for the powerful is still there in this passage from Isaiah. In Isaiah chapter three we have further parallel concepts with the blessings and woes of the Sermon on the Plain:

> The Lord rises to argue his case; he stands to judge the peoples. The Lord enters into judgment with the elders and princes of his people: It is you who have devoured the vineyard; the spoil of the poor is in your houses. What do you mean by crushing my people, by grinding the face of the poor? says the Lord God of hosts.
>
> The Lord said: Because the daughters of Zion are haughty and walk with outstretched necks, glancing wantonly with their eyes, mincing along as they go, tinkling with their feet; the Lord will afflict with scabs the heads of the daughters of Zion, and the Lord will lay bare their secret parts.
>
> In that day the Lord will take away the finery of the anklets, the headbands, and the crescents; the pendants, the bracelets, and the scarfs; the headdresses, the armlets, the sashes, the perfume boxes, and the amulets; the signet rings and nose rings; the festal

---

61. Bock, *The Theology of Luke and Acts,* 162.

> robes, the mantles, the cloaks, and the handbags; the garments
> of gauze, the linen garments, the turbans, and the veils. Instead
> of perfume there will be a stench; and instead of a sash, a rope;
> and instead of well-set hair, baldness; and instead of a rich robe, a
> binding of sackcloth; instead of beauty, shame. (Isa 3:13–24)

God, in this passage, is portrayed as a prosecuting attorney and judge, laying out his case against Judah and then prescribing the punishment. The case against Judah is that the rich and powerful engage in oppression and dispossession of the poor among them, while they themselves are haughty. The punishment is the absolute reversal of their fortunes. All the symbols of their wealth and power will be taken from them, even their beauty will be taken from them. It is a complete humiliation. One more passage in Isaiah that we will look at is found in chapter five:

> Ah, you who join house to house, who add field to field, until
> there is room for no one but you, and you are left to live alone in
> the midst of the land! The Lord of hosts has sworn in my hearing:
> Surely many houses shall be desolate, large and beautiful houses,
> without inhabitant. For ten acres of vineyard shall yield but one
> bath, and a homer of seed shall yield a mere ephah. (Isa 5:8–10)

In this passage we have judgment not only of wealth, but also of the accumulation of wealth, especially the accumulation of land—the primary source of wealth for agrarian societies. The judgment comes in the form of a foretelling of a reversal of fortunes: the rich who accumulate land will suffer loss, economic ruin, and ultimately death as we read further on in chapter five:

> Therefore my people go into exile without knowledge; their nobles
> are dying of hunger, and their multitude is parched with thirst.
> Therefore Sheol has enlarged its appetite and opened its mouth
> beyond measure; the nobility of Jerusalem and her multitude go
> down, her throng and all who exult in her. (Isa 5:13–14)

This foretelling of a reversal is in reference to the Babylonian exile.[62] Although the people are condemned to go into exile, the noblemen who ac-

---

62. Interestingly, Jeremiah 34:8–22 puts the cause of the Babylonian exile at the feet of those who did not correctly follow the Sabbatical Year law regulations related to releasing slaves. Combining Isaiah 5 with Jeremiah 34 allows us to say that there was a tradition of tying the exile to the Sabbatical and Jubilee regulations, since the kind of vast land accumulation Isaiah describes could only happen if the Jubilee was not followed. While Isaiah 5 blames the land accumulation, Jeremiah 34 blames the failure to release

cumulate wealth and land are judged harsher. The nobility are condemned to death, notably death by hunger; hunger being the very fate which the nobility condemned their fellow Israelites to when they accumulated more and more land, leaving less and less for the common Israelite.

Seeing the verses in Isaiah 10, 3, and 5 provides us with an explanation of the importance of the woes; it is not enough that the poor are relieved and given the Kingdom, the rich must be punished. The reason—although not explicit in the Sermon on the Plain, but which can be surmised from Isaiah, along with other prophetic texts in the Hebrew Bible—is that poverty and the suffering of poverty is a direct result of the oppression and dispossession by the rich of the poor. For the poor to be relieved, the rich must be stopped, and punished. Poverty in the prophetic tradition of the Hebrew bible is not a natural phenomenon, but it is the outcome of oppression, and the immoral actions of the rich and powerful.[63] The prophetic tradition in the Hebrew bible is full of these themes,[64] but this quick snapshot in Isaiah should suffice to provide us with a general picture to help us understand the prophetic background to the blessings and woes.

The prophetic tradition in the Hebrew bible was directly informed by the Torah. With regards to the blessings and woes of the Sermon on the Plain, the most important legislation would have to be the Jubilee law found in Leviticus 25. Like many ancient near eastern cultures and law codes, the Israelites and their Torah reflected a special concern for orphans, widows, and the poor in general. However, while most near eastern societies placed the responsibility (and praise) for caring for the poor on the kings; the Torah places that responsibility on everyone, and it also included outsiders—alien residents—in that obligation.[65] The logic for this concern is that God is on the side of the poor and therefore his people ought to be also.[66] With this background let us look at the Jubilee legislation found in Leviticus 25:10–55. This legislation was to be enacted every fifty years, after seven Sabbatical years.[67] The legislation commanded a release of all Israel-

---

slaves; but both tie the exile to a failure to follow the Sabbatical or Jubilee regulations.

63. Hoppe, *There Shall Be No Poor Among You*, 102.

64. Hoppe, *There Shall Be No Poor Among You*, 68.

65. Hoppe, *There Shall Be No Poor Among You*, 24–25.

66. Hoppe, *There Shall Be No Poor Among You*, 25. See Deuteronomy 10:14–19; 24:17–22 for examples of the logic of God's siding with the poor grounding the obligation of his people to care for the poor.

67. The Sabbatical year legislation found in Deuteronomy 15, which—as we will see below—is very relevant to understanding the ethics portion of the Sermon on the Plain.

ites in bond slavery, a ban on working the land during that year along with making the land and its produce available to everyone—making it common property—during that year, and a complete redistribution of the land back to the ancestral holdings of each family.[68] The theological Justification for this law is:

> The land shall not be sold in perpetuity, for the land is mine; with me you are but aliens and tenants. (Lev 25:23)

This legislation, like the prophetic tradition and the general trend in the Torah, grounded the concern for the poor in God himself. This legislation would completely reverse any move towards inequality or economic domination in Israel, and it provided the ideal: a society that reflected God's own justice and care for his people, and a society of solidarity in which everyone recognized their dependence on one another and recognized their obligations towards one another, and especially their complete dependence on God.[69]

The connection of the Jubilee (and Sabbatical) to both the prophetic tradition and the blessings and woes of the Sermon on the Plain should be clear. These legislations put forward the ideal of a just society—and when the society was not going in that direction, the prophets would call for the society to repent and follow God's requirements for a just society—but if they did not, then God would intervene in order to establish his requirements for a just society.

Poverty, Wealth, and Reversal in Hellenistic culture

The Hellenistic view of wealth was that wealth ought to be distributed according to virtue. In Aristotle's discussion of the "prodigal" type of person versus the "liberal" type of person he says:

> riches, therefore, will be used best by the man who has the virtue concerned with wealth; and this is the liberal man. Now spending and giving seem to be the using of wealth; taking and keeping

---

The Sabbatical year was held every seven years, and consisted of a releasing of all debts, and a releasing of those who had fallen into debt slavery. It also included a commandment to lend freely and generously to those in need, no matter how close the Sabbatical year was.

68. Hoppe, *There Shall Be No Poor Among You*, 32.

69. Hoppe, *There Shall Be No Poor Among You*, 32–33.

rather the possession of it. Hence it is more the mark of the liberal man to give to the right people than to take from the right sources and not to take from the wrong.

. . .

Hence also their giving [the prodigal men] is not liberal; for it is not noble, nor does it aim at nobility, nor is it done in the right way; sometimes they make rich those who should be poor, and will give nothing to people of respectable character. (Aristotle, *Ethics*, 4.1 [Ross])

The point Aristotle makes here is that the use of wealth must be in line with the virtues; and that according to one's virtue, one deserves either an increase of wealth, or to be poor. Poverty is a catastrophe when some people suffer it but warranted when others suffer it. This assumption is also found in Plato, in his political writings he disparages the concept of democracy for its tendency to give power to the poor. For example, in his work "The Republic" he writes:

And a democracy, I suppose, comes into being when the poor [οἱ πένητες, which as we mentioned above, refers more to the "working class" poor rather than the fully destitute πτωχοί], winning the victory, put to death some of the other party, drive out others, and grant the rest of the citizens an equal share in both citizenship and offices. (Plato, *Republic*, 8.557 [Grube and Reeve])

Plato envisions democracy as being the result of the poor, through the threat of violence, taking power and distributing it equally. According to Plato, democracy would lead to laziness, vice, and degeneracy. He describes the "democratic man" by saying:

he establishes and maintains all his pleasures on a footing of equality, forsooth, and so lives turning over the guard-house of his soul to each as it happens along until it is sated, as if it had drawn the lot for that office, and then in turn to another, disdaining none but fostering them all equally." "Quite so." "And he does not accept or admit into the guard-house the words of truth when anyone tells him that some pleasures arise from honorable and good desires, and others from those that are base, and that we ought to practice and esteem the one and control and subdue the others; but he shakes his head at all such admonitions and avers that they are all alike and to be equally esteemed." "Such is indeed his state of mind and his conduct." "And does he not," said I, "also live out his life in this fashion, day by day indulging the appetite of the day, now wine-bibbing and abandoning himself to the lascivious pleasing of the flute and again drinking only water and dieting; and at one time exercising his body, and sometimes idling and neglecting all things, and at another time seeming to occupy himself with philosophy. And frequently he goes in for politics and bounces up and says and does whatever enters his head. And if military men excite his emulation, thither he rushes, and if moneyed men, to that he turns, and there is no order or compulsion in his existence, but he calls this life of his the life of pleasure and freedom and happiness and cleaves to it to the end." "That is a perfect description," he said, "of a devotee of equality." (Plato, *Republic*, 8.561)

Plato basically argues here that the "democratic man"—which he is using as a personification of democracy as a political system—is whimsical; "he" goes after pleasure simply for pleasure's sake. The poor do not have the virtues necessary for proper government, they do not have the thrift of the moneyed men, nor the valor of the military man, nor the wisdom of the philosopher; rather, they just search for pleasure where ever it can be found. This is part of the reason Plato argues that democracy necessarily leads to tyranny (Plato, *Republic*, 8.562).

I would argue that both Plato and Aristotle would have been horrified by the blessings and woes of Jesus. The assured future Jesus was proclaiming would put the poor in charge over the rich; in fact, worse than that, it would be the destitute, the beggars, in charge, an even more terrifying thought than the working-class poor being in charge. This reversal would have the Kingdom of God in the hands of people who lacked virtue—demonstrated by the fact that they are destitute—and it would undo an order to the world that was justified and right. Plato might have even considered what Jesus was proclaiming to be a potentially disastrous move towards democracy, a move that could only result in tyranny.

Two philosophical currents that were rather popular around the time of Jesus were Epicureanism and Stoicism; both of which had a focus on ethics, including social ethics.

The basic Epicurean ethical framework was, in short, that the purpose of life was to maximize happiness, pleasure, or tranquility.[70] Naturally then, poverty for the Epicureans was in and of itself a negative; however, the solution for the poor (not necessarily the destitute) was to simply change one's expectation (Stobaeus, *Anthology*, 3.17.23). Poverty could, for Epicurus, be very well re-interpreted as being something positive:

70. Ferguson, *Backgrounds of Early Christianity*, 375.

Poverty, if measured by the natural end, is great wealth; but wealth, if not limited, is great poverty. (Epicurus, *Vatican Sayings,* 26[Geer])

This re-interpretation of poverty is common in Greek philosophy and can be seen clearly in Xenophon's Economics:

"And in spite of that estimate, you really think you have no need of money and pity me for my poverty?"

Yes, because my property is sufficient to satisfy my wants, but I don't think you would have enough to keep up the style you are living in and to support your reputation, even if your fortune were three times what it is." (Xenophon, *Oeconomicus,* 2.4 [Heinemann])

The idea here is that poverty is no big problem as long as one's desires for wealth are in line with what one has; and that riches can be a problem if they are accompanied with a desire for more wealth. The point is that one simply needs to adjust one's expectation to alleviate much of the suffering that comes from poverty.

Stoic Ethics had somewhat different assumptions. The goal of the Stoics was to live in accord with nature.[71] This view also allowed for the normalization of poverty. For example, according to Seneca:

"Poverty brought into conformity with the law of nature, is great wealth." Do you know what limits that law of nature ordains for us? Merely to avert hunger, thirst, and cold.

. . .

He who has made a fair compact with poverty is rich. (Seneca, *Moral Epistles to Lucilius,* 4.10–12 [Gummere])

Here we have the basic Stoic *apologia* for poverty: if you are poor, as long as your poverty is in line with the natural order, just make peace with it.

Both the Epicureans and the Stoics would take issue with Jesus's declaration of an eschatological reversal. The Epicureans might say that this apocalyptic dream will end up causing more suffering: causing suffering for the rich, and even for the poor in that the hope for a reversal will cause them to desire riches. Stoics might protest that dreaming of an eschatological reversal is a disordered desire to overthrow nature, and evidence that Jesus and his followers were unable to live in accordance with the logic of the natural order.

---

71. Ferguson, *Backgrounds of Early Christianity,* 359.

Summation

The vision of Jesus strongly differs from the Hellenistic norm, as well as some strands of Judaism. Rather than seeing poverty as a reflection of bad character, or as something that could be justified as acceptable; Jesus portrays it as something bad, horrible even; but he also places God on the side of the poor, along with the promise of an eschatological reversal. The rich on the other hand are going to lose what they have; their wealth is not a reflection of any virtue but rather the result of the corrupt system of things which God will reverse. Jesus's vision is apocalyptic and eschatological, and as such fits in with a prophetic tradition within Judaism. Jesus then addresses the audience and presents them with a choice: they can be on the side of the poor in the eschatological reversal and suffer persecution in this system of things; or they can be well spoken of in this system of things and be on the side of the rich in the eschatological reversal. In presenting them with that choice he also reminds them of the historical prophetic tradition: how the prophets were abused in their own time, yet how they were on the side of righteousness. The vision here is counter to Hellenistic common sense, philosophical currents, some pharisaic thought, and some of the Jewish wisdom tradition; but attaches itself very nicely to the apocalyptic, eschatological, and prophetic tradition within Judaism.

4

The Ethics

FOLLOWING THE BLESSINGS AND woes is the meat of the Sermon on the Plain: The Ethics (Luke 6:27–38). Before we look at the ethical section of the Sermon, let us take a look at some currents within Hellenistic social ethical thought that were relevant to the world of Jesus.

Plato and Aristotle

Plato's and Aristotle's general method when thinking of social ethics was that the goal of social ethics was to create a "just" society where everything was in its correct place as its nature dictated, so that society could run in a virtuous way. In both Plato's and Aristotle's writings we find the common Hellenistic concept of "friendship" as holding all things in common—this is the ideal for both of them (Plato, *Republic*, 5.449c; Aristotle, *Ethics*, 8.1). Friendship in the Greco-Roman world was of upmost importance: it was the ideal social relationship; however, it was not thought to be universally applicable: it depended on the participants being social equals.[1] We see this in both Plato and Aristotle. For example, in Plato's Laws it says:

> For slaves will never be friends with masters, nor bad men with good, even when they occupy equal positions—for when equality is given to unequal things, the resultant will be unequal

1. Ferguson, *Backgrounds of Early Christianity*, 67–68.

. . .

but the truest and best form of equality is not an easy thing for
everyone to discern. It is the judgment of Zeus, and men it never
assists save in small measure, but in so far as it does assist either
States or individuals, it produces all things good; for it dispenses
more to the greater and less to the smaller, giving due measure
to each according to nature; and with regard to honors also, by
granting the greater to those that are greater in goodness, and the
less to those of the opposite character in respect of goodness and
education, it assigns in proportion what is fitting to each. Indeed,
it is precisely this which constitutes for us "political justice," (Plato,
Laws, 6.756e–6.757c [Saunders])

Aristotle echoes the sentiment by saying:

Differences arise also in friendships based on superiority; for each
expects to get more out of them, but when this happens the friendship is dissolved. Not only does the better man think he ought to
get more, since more should be assigned to a good man, but the
more useful similarly expects this; they say a useless man should
not get as much as they should, since it becomes an act of public
service and not a friendship if the proceeds of the friendship do
not answer to the worth of the benefits conferred. For they think
that, as in a commercial partnership those who put more in get
more out, so it should be in friendship. But the man who is in a
state of need and inferiority makes the opposite claim; they think
it is the part of a good friend to help those who are in need; what,
they say, is the use of being the friend of a good man or a powerful
man, if one is to get nothing out of it? (Aristotle, *Ethics*, 8.14)

Here we see in both Plato and Aristotle the Hellenistic view of fairness and
justice: there is no equality, and distribution should be made in terms of
merit. The virtuous and noble, the powerful and aristocratic, ought to have
more than the un-virtuous and common, because the former deserve it.
This is why there can be no sharing, or real friendship, between the higher
and lower classes. Sharing between classes would give to the undeserving
what rightly belongs to the deserving. This tendency of thought gives us a
kind of meritocracy; but for Plato "merit" is measured according to one's
"nature" (φύσις) and one's "honors" (τιμή), and for Aristotle it is the better
(βελτίων) and superior (εὐεργεσίας) versus the useless (ἀχρεῖος) and needy
(ἐνδείας).

This way of thinking defined the Greco-Roman world, every individual had his value, his honor, and should be treated accordingly.

Friendship was for equals, but for Plato and Aristotle, many people with whom we interact are not our equal. For unequals we need "society," or the *polis*, rather than friendship. In Plato's Republic, before laying out his vision of a perfect city, he gives a theory on the origin of society saying:

> I think a city comes to be because none of us is self-sufficient, but we all need many things. Do you think that a city is founded on any other principle?
>
> No.
>
> And because people need many things, and because one person calls on a second out of one need and on a third out of a differ-ent need, many people gather in a single place to live together as partners and helpers. And such a settlement is called a city. Isn't that so?
>
> It is.
>
> And if they share things with one another, giving and taking, they do so because each believes that this is better for himself? (Plato, *Republic*, 2.369b–c)

The assumption here is that a society is based primarily on self-interest: every person has various needs and wants, which he cannot fulfill himself; therefore, people need to come together and interact for the sake of survival and mutual benefit. The result of this is the creation of a market system in society:

> And how will those in the city itself share the things that each produces?
>
> It was for the sake of this that we made their partnership and founded their city.
>
> Clearly, they must do it by buying and selling.
>
> Then we'll need a marketplace and a currency for such exchange.
>
> Certainly.
>
> If a farmer or any other craftsman brings some of his products to market, and he doesn't arrive at the same time as those who want to exchange things with him, is he to sit idly in the marketplace, away from his own work?

Not at all. There'll be people who'll notice this and provide the requisite service—in well-organized cities they'll usually be those whose bodies are weakest and who aren't fit to do any other work. They'll stay around the market exchanging money for the goods of those who have something to sell and then exchanging those goods for the money of those who want them.

Then, to fill this need there will have to be retailers in our city, for aren't those who establish themselves in the marketplace to provide this service of buying and selling called retailers, while those who travel between cities are called merchants?

That's right.

There are other servants, I think, whose minds alone wouldn't qualify them for membership in our society but whose bodies are strong enough for labor. These sell the use of their strength for a price called a wage and hence are themselves called wage-earners. Isn't that so?

Certainly.

So wage-earners complete our city?

I think so. (Plato, *Republic*, 2.371b–e)

This long passage basically follows the standard market logic: people get together for reasons of self-interest, and therefore contract with each other back and forth in order to service their self-interest in the marketplace. In the end, through market mechanisms, everyone finds their place in society based on their merit, on their characteristics.

The same sentiment is given by Aristotle:

Now all forms of community are like parts of the political community; for men journey together with a view to some particular advantage, and to provide something that they need for the purposes of life; (Aristotle, *Ethics*, 8.8)

Again, we see that it is the mutual benefit of the various parties that leads to the forming of communities. Aristotle, along with Plato, sees this as the origin of markets. For Aristotle, markets come about so as to make sure that goods being distributed are done so fairly. For this to happen we need currency—which is the mediation between goods—which ensures that the goods traded are of proportional value so that both parties come out happy. Aristotle writes:

For it is not two doctors that associate for exchange, but a doctor and a farmer, or in general people who are different and unequal; but these must be equated. This is why all things that are exchanged must be somehow comparable. It is for this end that money has been introduced, and it becomes in a sense an intermediate; for it measures all things,

. . .

If it had not been possible for reciprocity to be thus effected, there would have been no association of the parties. That demand holds things together as a single unit is shown by the fact that when men do not need one another, i.e., when neither needs the other or one does not need the other, they do not exchange, (Aristotle, *Ethics*, 5.5)

Aristotle, like Plato, has a very familiar notion of the market: people come together because they want to get something out of each other, and calculated exchanges facilitate that. The market is separate from friendship, which is among social equals who are virtuous. However, the assumptions are the same, all social interaction depends on some personal benefit, even if that benefit is something like virtue. Plato puts it this way:

Someone who is both believed to be useful and is useful is a friend; someone who is believed to be useful but isn't, is believed to be a friend but isn't. And the same for the enemy. (Plato, *Republic*, 1.334e)

For Aristotle friendship should not be based on pure utility, but he thinks that love ought to only be for good virtuous people:

But if one accepts another man as good, and he turns out badly and is seen to do so, must one still love him? Surely it is impossible, since not everything can be loved, but only what is good.

. . .

But if one friend remained the same while the other became better and far outstripped him in virtue, should the latter treat the former as a friend? Surely he cannot. (Aristotle, *Ethics*, 4.3)

A friend is one that is your equal, a friend—one that you love—is someone who will better you and be beneficial to you. We have a basic idea laid out that people are simply not equal—one's affections belong to those who are equal, and we can share goods and love in common with those who are equal to us; for the rest, we have society—where people interact based on self-interest—and from society we have market transactions (among other institutions such as slavery, political power, and so on).

The Epicureans and the Stoics

Epicurus's social ethics, or politics, is quite similar to some of the political theories developed in the modern period: it is based around the idea of a social contract rooted in individual self-interest. For Epicurus, justice was just an expedient way to maximize pleasure, and was more or less contract based:

> There never was an absolute justice, but only an agreement made in reciprocal intercourse in whatever localities now and again from time to time, providing against the infliction or suffering of harm.
> . . .
> Taken generally, justice is the same for all, to wit, something found expedient in mutual intercourse. (Laertius, *Lives of Eminent Philosophers*, 10.150–151 [Hicks])

This way of thinking rings familiar to modern western ears, it fits with enlightenment and post-enlightenment social contract theory as well as the modern market ideology. For the Epicureans, the main ethical *telos* was tranquility, happiness, and especially pleasure—on an individual level. Out of this starting point comes the social theory: if each person is individually seeking to maximize his individual wellbeing, then each person would associate with his neighbor in such a way so as to enhance that wellbeing. Community for the Epicureans was a means to an end.[2] With the assumption of an inherently self-interested individual, it becomes easy to see why ethics becomes a matter of contract, and why justice becomes the ability to form contracts that maximize utility.[3]

For the Epicureans, justice was merely contractual and relative: there is no higher transcendent good being served, justice is merely a way for individuals to maximize their pleasure.[4] The same is true of friendship. Friendship was held in very high esteem by the Epicureans, as one of the highest goods; however, the point of friendship was personal security, as

---

2. Ferguson, *Backgrounds of Early Christianity*, 375–377.
3. Long and Sedley, *The Hellenistic Philosophies: Volume 1*, 134–135.
4. O'keefe, *Epicureanism*, 141–142.

well as mutual aid and personal enrichment.[5] Maximizing pleasure is virtually impossible if you have to fend for yourself, emotionally, physically, or intellectually; therefore, cultivating and maintaining friendships is one of the highest epicurean values. Cicero, in explaining a prominent Epicurean view of friendship, writes:

> It affords us enjoyment in the present, and it inspires us with hopes for the near and distant future. Thus it is not possible to secure uninterrupted gratification in life without friendship, nor yet to preserve friendship itself unless we love our friends as much as ourselves. (Cicero, *De Finibus I, 67* [Rackham])

Thus friendship, although not contractual like justice, still maintains the Epicurean orthodoxy of the individual pursuit of pleasure, even if in manifests in a seemingly altruistic and unselfish way.

Stoic social ethics focused much on a conformity to nature. This focus led to a philosophy of equality. The argument for Stoic equality goes something like this: all men have possession of a divine *logos* (or reason), this gives them the power to conform to nature, which gives them ethical worth, therefore all men ought to have equal status, since their value (along with their *telos*) comes from their possession of the *logos*.[6] Because all men have this reason and equality, they have moral obligations to one another; this community of reason is in a sense *a priori*—not contractual—and transcendent.[7] In this view of society, serving one another is not done for the sake of one another, or for the sake of yourself; but rather for the sake of the higher good: the natural order.

Friendship for the Stoics, like the Epicureans, was held in very high esteem; but it was based on virtue and wisdom. Friendship was dependent on a shared set of values, a shared purpose.[8] However, friendship was to be kept in check. One should, according to the Stoics, never become so attached to someone that he or she could threaten your serenity. The Stoic philosopher Epictetus, writing on the dangers of friendship says:

> First of all the highest and the principal, and that which stands as it were at the entrance, is this; when you are delighted with anything, be delighted as with a thing which is not one of those which

---

5. O'keefe, *Epicureanism*, 147–148.

6. Colish, *The Stoic Tradition*, 36–37.

7. Colish, *The Stoic Tradition*, 38.

8. Colish, *The Stoic Tradition*, 42.

cannot be taken away, but as with something of such a kind, as an earthen pot is, or a glass cup, that when it has been broken, you may remember what it was, and may not be troubled. So in this matter also: if you kiss your own child, or your brother or friend, never give full license to the appearance, and allow not your pleasure to go as far as it chooses; but check it, and curb it as those who stand behind men in their triumphs and remind them that they are mortal. (Epictetus, *Discourses III,* 24 [Oldfather])

Stoicism differed very much with Epicureanism when it came to the purposes of social relationships. For example, when it came to benefaction, the stoics were clear that it was not to be based in self-interest. On benefaction (which we will shortly talk about in slightly more detail) Seneca writes:

For if we look at everything merely from the point of view of our intentions, every man has done as much as he chose to do; and since filial piety, good faith, justice, and in short every virtue is complete within itself, a man may be grateful in intention even though he may not be able to lift a hand to prove his gratitude. Whenever a man obtains what he aimed at, he receives the fruit of his labor. When a man bestows a benefit, at what does he aim? Clearly to be of service and afford pleasure to him upon whom he bestows it. If he does what he wishes, if his purpose reaches me and fills us each with joy, he has gained his object. He does not wish anything to be given to him in return, or else it becomes an exchange of commodities, not a bestowal of benefits. (Seneca, *On Benefits II,* 31 [Stewart])

The point was that, for the Stoics, the motivation for moral action was just as important as the action itself. In social ethics, mutual aid and cooperation was to be done for its own sake, and for the sake of virtue; if it was not, then it was not counted as a social good. The point of all of this is that human life must not be about pleasure, selfish happiness, or anything like that; rather, it must be a conformity to nature, a dispassionate embrace of virtue.

One of the most important social institutions in the Greco-Roman world was benefaction, also known as patronage. This relationship was one in which a wealthy patron, or benefactor, would provide money, goods, or protection to his poorer clients who would reciprocate by providing the patron with honor, service, and loyalty.[9] The logic here was that of an exchange: material aid in exchange for honor. It was both a vertical relationship, entirely based on the inequality of the patron and client; and also an

---

9. Ferguson, *Backgrounds of Early Christianity,* 67.

exchange in which both parties had obligations and claims in relation to the other party.[10] This would require however, for the client to have some honor to give; because of this, a poor client would have to be the "right" kind of poor person: a citizen, or a poor person with some social standing.[11] Therefore this kind of patronage was not available for the truly poor and destitute,[12] a category that—for the Greco-Roman world—was almost subhuman, not worth any concern, and not of any moral value.[13] This attitude even applied to the generally more humanitarian philosophers.[14]

This institution puts a spotlight on just how important the concept of honor was in the Greco-Roman world. This world was not a guilt culture; but rather an honor culture where your standing was measured against public opinion. Even among the moral teachers, it was common to judge conduct as honorable or dishonorable rather than right or wrong. What was honorable in the Greco-Roman world was that which preserved and enhanced the correct order and stability of society; shame was that which undermined that order and stability. Honor also came from being born to a high-status family, or from simply being wealthy; acts of courage and benevolence were also deemed honorable (as they enhanced the stability of the Greco-Roman order).[15]

The Ethics of Jesus

The ethics portion of the Sermon on the Plain can be broken up into the commandments (27–31), the rhetorical questions explaining the commandments (32–35), and the commandments with their rewards (36–38). The central theme of the ethics is a rejection of the principle of reciprocity,[16] and a mandate for principles of excessive generosity, community, and non-retaliation.

10. Malina, *The Social World of Jesus and the Gospels*, 144.

11. Morely, "The poor in the city of Rome," in Atkins and Osborne, *Poverty in the Roman world*, 34.

12. Woolfe, "Writing Poverty in Rome," in Atkins and Osborne, *Poverty in the Roman world*, 85.

13. Woolfe, "Writing Poverty in Rome," in Atkins and Osborne, *Poverty in the Roman world*, 99.

14. Parkin, "You do him no Service," in Atkins and Osborne, *Poverty in the Roman world*, 68.

15. Ferguson, *Backgrounds of Early Christianity*, 69.

16. Talbert, *Reading Luke*, 75–77.

27–31

Beginning the ethics section is a rather bold statement (27); one which can be described as the authoritative doctrine of Jesus:[17]

> But to YOU, to those listening, I say—love YOUR enemies, do good to those hating YOU.
>
> Ἀλλ' ὑμῖν λέγω τοῖς ἀκούουσιν· ἀγαπᾶτε τοὺς ἐχθροὺς ὑμῶν, καλῶς ποιεῖτε τοῖς μισοῦσιν ὑμᾶς,

The transition phrase "But to YOU, to those listening" (Ἀλλ' ὑμῖν λέγω τοῖς ἀκούουσιν), indicates that Jesus is addressing the crowd: his would-be disciples—the audience of the fourth blessing and woe—with the meat of the Sermon: the ethics.[18] One indication connecting verse 27 to the last blessing and woe is the usage of the phrase "μισοῦσιν ὑμᾶς;" Jesus says that his disciples—those on the side of "the destitute"—will be hated. Following that declaration, he, right at the beginning of his ethical treatise, commands them to do good to the ones hating them.[19] This connection is in fact an indication that Luke may be recording an oral form of the speech; rather than arranging disperse written material,[20] and is further evidence that the blessings and woes did not circulate independently from the ethics portion of the Sermon.

We see in verse 27 two parallel commandments: love your enemies, do good to those that hate you. The implication here is that "to love" (ἀγαπάω), is interchangeable with "doing good" (καλῶς ποιεῖν); and that "enemies" (εχθροί) are defined as the ones that hate you (μισοῦσιν ὑμᾶς).[21] Getting these definitions clear is important for what follows in the Sermon. For Jesus, love is not an emotion or simply an inclination of the heart, it is a tangible and visible practice.[22] Likewise, enemies are not necessarily those whom the listener deems to be his enemy; but rather those who deem him to be their enemy.

17. Betz, *A commentary on the Sermon on the Mount, including the Sermon on the Plain*, 592.

18. Fitzmyer, *The Gospel According to Luke I–IX*, 637.

19. Fitzmyer, *The Gospel According to Luke I–IX*, 637.

20. Marshall, *The Gospel of Luke*, 259.

21. Betz, *A commentary on the Sermon on the Mount, including the Sermon on the Plain*, 592.

22. Marshall, *The Gospel of Luke*, 259; Evans, *Saint Luke*, 334.

Compared with the epicurean or stoic view of social ethics, we have something completely out of the ordinary. Far from being a mutually beneficial contract (Epicureanism), love and good works are given without any guarantee of benefit; in fact, the opposite of a guaranteed benefit seems likely. Also, this does not seem at all to be in line with nature or with limiting one's suffering (Stoicism); this kind of moral stance seems to go against the natural order of things (the natural order of things being that your love is appropriate for those who love you) and seems to exasperate the risk of suffering. The fact that this kind of love is commanded puts a gulf between Jesus's ethics and the Stoic and Epicurean ethics. The Hellenistic philosophical tradition could perhaps have room for attempting to turn enemies into friends; but certainly not commanding the love of enemies no matter the conditions and with no caveat.[23]

The Sermon on the Mount and the *Didache* (texts that seem to be more Jewish focused than Luke) provide some clarification for this commandment.[24] The Sermon on the Mount ties this commandment with a saying which apparently comes from an older Jewish tradition:

> "You have heard that it was said, 'You shall love your neighbor and hate your enemy.' But I say to you, Love your enemies and pray for those who persecute you, (Matt 5:43–44)

The first part of the commandment—"love your neighbor"—comes from Leviticus 19[25]:

> And your own hand shall not take vengeance, and you shall not be angry against the sons of your people, and you shall love your neighbor as yourself; it is I who am the Lord. (Lev 19:18 [NETS])

Although Matthew explicitly quotes Leviticus 19:18 (perhaps explaining the original saying) and Luke does not; the echo of Leviticus 19:18 is certainly there in Luke 6:27, even though it is there as an inversion (love your enemies rather than love your neighbor).[26] The closest thing we have in ancient Jewish tradition to the saying "hate your enemy" is found in the Community Rule document among the Qumran scrolls:

23. Fitzmyer, *The Gospel According to Luke I–IX*, 637–638.

24. Betz, *A commentary on the Sermon on the Mount, including the Sermon on the Plain*, 70; Shawn, "Didache," in Barry, *The Lexham Bible Dictionary*.

25. From here forward all quotations from the Hebrew bible will be from the Greek translation of the Septuagint (the LXX), with English translation from the NETS.

26. Allison, *Constructing Jesus*, 353.

> He commanded by the hand of Moses and all His servants the
> Prophets; that they may love all that He has chosen and hate all
> that He has rejected
>
> . . .
>
> that they may love all the sons of light, each according to his
> lot in God's design, and hate all the sons of darkness, each accord-
> ing to his guilt in God's vengeance. (1QS 1.1)

For the community of the Community Rule document, hatred is appropriate for those whom God hates, whom God has rejected. In the context of the
Community Rule audience, the object of hatred would be the Kittim (the
gentile oppressors of the Jews), and the Jews who collaborate with them.

If this is the correct context, then the identity of the enemy in the
Sermon on the Plain—from a historical standpoint—is clear; these are not
simply people who hate Jesus's audience; these are the oppressors of Jesus's
audience, the imperial overlords and their Aristocratic/High Priestly al-
lies.[27] Given the later history of Judea and Galilee, with the Zealot war and
the eventual destruction of Jerusalem by the Roman army, this might have
been practical advice; but if it was, it was only retrospectively so, at the time
it would have seemed both counter-intuitive and somewhat dishonorable.

27. Richard Horsley disputes this interpretation (Horsley, *Jesus and the Spiral of Violence,* 260–267) on the basis that in other places in the Synoptics (Matthew 13:25, 28,
39; 10:34–36; 22:44; Luke 10:19; 20:43; 23:12) the term enemy (εχθρος) does not always
refer to a political enemy, but is often a personal enemy, or even Satan. I do not follow
Horsley's conclusion here for the following reasons:
    1. In the parable of the sower (found in Matthew 13) the personal enemy who sows
weeds, is compared to Satan, that does not mean that Satan can be thought of as a non-
political enemy, what it means is that Jesus is recorded by Matthew as using an example
of a personal enemy (the sower of weeds) to make a point about Satan, who was certainly
conceived of as a political enemy in opposition to God's Kingdom (Luke 4:5–8; 11:17–20;
Mark 3:23–26; Matthew 4:8–10; 12:25–27; Revelation 2:13; 2 Corinthians 4:4; Ephesians
2:2; John 14:30; 1 John 5:19; Barnabas 18.1–2; Martyrdom of Polycarp 2.4) and especially
so in some of the Qumran documents where Belial is identified with, and as, a political
enemy—such as 1QS (the Community Rule Document), CD (the Damascus Document),
and 1QM (The War Scroll). So that parable does not rule out that εχθρος in the Sermon
refers to political enemies.
    2. The commandment from the Torah being referred to in Luke 6:27 is Leviticus
19:18, in which the commandment is to love your neighbour, neighbour being the fellow Israelite. Had εχθρος in the Sermon referred to a fellow Israelite who was a personal
enemy, Jesus would just have been repeating the commandment in Leviticus 19:18 using
different language, it would have been a tautology, since loving neighbors (fellow Israelites) would only need to be a commandment if it included those who one might want to
consider a personal enemy. Given the allusion to Leviticus 19:18, the interpretation of
εχθρος as non-Israelite, political enemies must remain a plausible interpretation.

The *Didache* also sheds some light on this commandment by adding a few words of explanation:

> But you must love those who hate you, and you will not have an enemy. (Didache 1.3 [Holmes])

This gives the commandment a kind of practical logic: if you love your enemy, eventually he will not be your enemy, you will win him over as a friend. This logic works when the two parties are more or less equal in power; but when one is a domineering oppressor, such as the Roman occupiers, and the other is the oppressed, such as the Galilean and Judean people, things are rather different. Showing love to an oppressor is perhaps more likely to reinforce the oppressor's ability to justify his oppression than it is to convince the oppressor to cease his oppression. As we continue reading however, we will see further indications that Jesus's commandment is not limited to enemies of equal power.

Moving on to verses 28–29 we see examples of how this commandment could play out:

> Bless those cursing YOU, pray for those who insult YOU. To the one striking you on the cheek, offer also the other; and from the one taking your coat, do not hold back even your tunic.
>
> εὐλογεῖτε τοὺς καταρωμένους ὑμᾶς, προσεύχεσθε περὶ τῶν ἐπηρεαζόντων ὑμᾶς. τῷ τύπτοντί σε ἐπὶ τὴν σιαγόνα πάρεχε καὶ τὴν ἄλλην, καὶ ἀπὸ τοῦ αἴροντός σου τὸ ἱμάτιον καὶ τὸν χιτῶνα μὴ κωλύσῃς.

The first commandment is echoed elsewhere in the New Testament,[28] the idea being that when someone has malicious intentions towards you, you respond with a blessing. The word for "curse" (καταράομαι) could have the implication of the use of magic,[29] which one is to respond to with a "blessing," rather than a counter curse. This kind of blessing that has the implication of the use of magic however, has no Jewish antecedents, it would seem to be a borrowed gentile concept (if it be this kind of blessing Jesus is referring to).[30] More likely Jesus has in mind the kind of blessing which does have Jewish antecedents, such as the kind of blessing we see in the story of Balaam, where his curse is turned into a blessing by God (Num

---

28. For example see Romans 12:14, 17; 1 Corinthians 4:12; 1 Peter 3:9.

29. Betz, *A commentary on the Sermon on the Mount, including the Sermon on the Plain*, 594.

30. Marshall, *The Gospel of Luke*, 259.

22:41–24:9). Cursing in this context may not just refer to using strong language to condemn someone, but rather to appealing to spiritual powers to harm someone; this "cursing" is, in a sense, an initiation of violence. This is followed by the command to "pray" for those who abuse you, this goes contrary to the reflexive response of the abused to appeal to a higher power for retribution; such as was the reflex of the disciples James and John in Luke 9:54[31] when a village of Samaritans did not receive Jesus:

> When his disciples James and John saw it, they said, "Lord, do you want us to command fire to come down from heaven and consume them?"

Jesus's response, consistent with his teaching in the Sermon, was to rebuke his disciples for having that reflex. The phrase "insult YOU" (ἐπηρεαζόντων ὑμᾶς) can also mean "abuse YOU," or "molest YOU," making it fit more along the lines of general persecution.[32] The response Jesus commands is to pray for those abusing you, foreshadowing Jesus's appeal to his father at Golgotha:[33]

> Then Jesus said, "Father, forgive them; for they do not know what they are doing." (Luke 23:34)

Verse 29 in the Sermon gives us concrete examples of two kinds of abuse: humiliating violence, and theft. The first, the famous turn the other cheek commandment, has Halachic implications; in the Baba Kamma tractate of the Mishnah we read a ruling on being slapped:

> If a man cuffed or [punched] his fellow he must pay him a *sela* [4 zuz]. Rabbi Judah says in the name of Rabbi Jose the Galilean: One hundred *zuz*. If he slapped him he must pay 200 *zuz*. If [he struck him] with the back of his hand he must pay him 400 *zuz*. (Mishnah, *Baba Kamma*. 8.6)

This brings Jesus's commandment into the real world of first-century Judea and Galilee. A slap was considered worse than being punched, likely because of the indignity implied with a slap meant to humiliate rather than a punch meant to harm.[34] But a slap with the backhand implied a double indignity. One interpretation of Jesus's commandment of offering

---

31. This pericope is only found in Luke.
32. Marshall, *The Gospel of Luke*, 260.
33. This saying is only found in Luke.
34. See Mishnah, *Baba Kamma*. 8.1.

the other cheek is that the victim of an indignity ought to subject himself to potentially double the indignity. Being slapped across the face was also considered to be extremely undignified in the Hellenistic world—a real life example of this can be found in Tacitus's account of Sejanus's revenge on Drusus:

> Drusus, who could not brook a rival and was somewhat irascible, had, in a casual dispute, raised his fist at Sejanus, and, when he defended himself, had struck him in the face. On considering every plan, Sejanus thought his easiest revenge was to turn his attention to Livia, Drusus's wife. (Tacitus, *Annals*, 4.3 [Church and Brodribb])
>
> . . .
>
> Sejanus accordingly thought that he must be prompt, and chose a poison the gradual working of which might be mistaken for a natural disorder. It was given to Drusus by Lygdus, a eunuch, as was ascertained eight years later. (Tacitus, *Annals*, 4.8)

For Sejanus, being struck on the face by Drusus was such a horrific insult—such an indignity—that it drove him to hatch an elaborate plan to destroy Drusus, involving the seduction of his wife, and eventually his poisoning. The concept of indignity also applies to the second commandment in verse 29, which says that if your coat is stolen, by robbery, you are to let the robber have even your shirt.[35] These two forms of humiliation being thought of together—robbery and physical assault—would not be completely out of place in Hellenistic thought. In Plato's Gorgias we see them put together in a discussion about indignity between Callicles and Socrates, in which Socrates argues against what seems to be a commonly held view on what are the greatest indignities:

> I deny, Callicles, that to be wrongfully boxed on the ear is the deepest disgrace, or to have either my person cut or my purse; I hold that to strike or cut me or mine wrongfully is yet more of a disgrace and an evil, and likewise stealing and kidnapping and housebreaking, and in short any wrong whatsoever done to me or mine, are both worse and more shameful to the wrongdoer than to me the wronged. (Plato, *Gorgias*, 508 D–E [Zeyl])

Socrates here is making the point that the abuser is actually more shameful than the abused; but for the sake of the Sermon on the Plain the point is

---

35. Evans, *Saint Luke*, 335.

clear: being hit on the face, or being robbed, are among the deepest forms of humiliation. The reason for this is also laid out by Plato:

> And yet what wisdom is there, Socrates, "in an art that found a man of goodly parts and made him worse," unable either to succor himself, or to deliver himself or anyone else from the greatest dangers, but like to be stripped by his enemies of all his substance, and to live in his city as an absolute outcast? Such a person, if one may use a rather low expression, can be given a box on the ear with impunity. (Plato, *Gorgias*, 486 B–C)

The reason being slapped in the face, or robbed, is so shameful is because it demonstrates that one is defenseless, that one cannot stand up for one's self, that one is vulnerable and weak. In this sense the slapping is really the initiation of a game, a game in which the reputation of the challenger and challenged is at stake.[36] Loss of honor is, in cultures dominated by violence, systemic or otherwise, (as was the Roman world), often a justification for violence and oppression.[37] Gaining honor brought with it entitlement to worth and status;[38] if honor is lost however, the only way it can be regained is by, in a sense, playing the game of the people who took your honor from you, according to David Graeber:

> honor is, by definition, something that exists in the eyes of others. To be able to recover it, then, a slave must necessarily adopt the rules and standards of the society that surrounds him, and this means that, in practice at least, he cannot absolutely reject the institutions that deprived him of his honor in the first place.[39]

To retaliate against an act of violence meant to humiliate in order to restore one's honor would, in effect, be justifying the concept of honor as something which needs to be maintained by violence. Since honor was really just another word for social value in many ancient mediterranean cultures,[40] retaliation would basically justify the status quo of violence as being one of the main means of establishing human value and dignity.

Violence, above and beyond all other forms of human interaction, is really a form of stupidity—not only in that it is a stupid way of handling

---

36. Malina, *The New Testament World*, 35–36.
37. Graeber, *Debt*, 166.
38. Malina, *The New Testament World*, 31–32.
39. Graeber, *Debt*, 167.
40. Malina, *The New Testament World*, 29.

problems—but more concretely in that it erases from the interaction any meaning or necessity of understanding. David Graeber writes:

> Violence's capacity to allow arbitrary decisions, and thus to avoid the kind of debate, clarification, and renegotiation typical of more egalitarian social relations, is obviously what allows its victims to see procedures created on the basis of violence as stupid or unreasonable.[41]
>
> . . .
>
> violence may well be the only way it is possible for one human being to do something which will have relatively predictable effects on the actions of a person about whom they understand nothing. In pretty much any other way in which you might try to influence another's actions, you must at least have some idea about who you think they are, who they think you are, what they might want out of the situation, their aversions and proclivities, and so forth. Hit them over the head hard enough, and all of this becomes irrelevant.[42]

In striking someone on the face, one is basically making a claim that the victim can be manipulated without any communication, simply with the threat of violence, and that the victim lacks dignity: he is not worth communicating with. The victim is now in a situation where communication has been banished and his only remaining options are to strike back to maintain his honor—which may lead to further violence—showing that he cannot be manipulated with merely the threat of force; or he could simply take the indignity and hope it does not have any further consequences. Jesus's solution however, is to not accept the rules. In fact, his solution is to completely invert the rules.

In offering the other cheek the victim does something completely unexpected to the perpetrator: he invites further humiliating violence, he does so without fear, and he does so explicitly. At this point the perpetrator would be forced to realize that his violence has failed: it did not strip the honor from the victim, and the victim cannot be manipulated through violence.

In rejecting violent retaliation, Jesus is also rejecting a type of moral foundation of social relationships based on exchange. Violence is not only a breakdown of communication and an attempt at manipulation without personal insight, it is also a kind of exchange relationship. Far from being

41. Graeber, *Utopia of Rules*, 41.
42. Graeber, *Utopia of Rules*, 42.

the result of a breakdown of social cohesion based on exchange, it is often used as a social tool in order to maintain an equilibrium of order.[43] In violent situations where the victor is not yet clear (so for example, two people on the street having a fist fight; as opposed to a master beating a slave), the situation is usually thought of as a competitive exchange, similar to how one speaks of market competition.[44] In a society where honor is thought of as extremely significant, games of exchange—be they physical combat, or even a game of who can give the largest gift—become very important in establishing one's place in the hierarchy of honor.[45] Therefore we can say that violence—at least some kinds of violence, in a martial, honor based society, such as the Roman society—was an integral part of the maintaining of order. Beyond merely keeping the subject population in line, violence established position and honor; and made sure that one's position in society was clear relative to everyone else's.

If one is challenged to a "game of honor," such as by being struck on the face, the rules of tit-for-tat exchange immediately come into play, and one is obligated to repay the challenge in order to maintain one's honor, and one must continue the game until it is resolved.[46] By turning the other cheek, the victim neither concedes subjugation—since he is maintaining his agency and responding in a way that makes it clear that he is neither afraid nor willing to have his actions dictated by his assailant—nor does he respond in an equivalent way so as to continue the game of honor, which would be tacitly acknowledging the game.

An interesting aspect of verse 29 is the switch from the second person plural to the second person singular. Some have suggested that this shows evidence that multiple traditions are being brought together; but it is more likely the case that we are moving from collective, more general, commandments to individual, more specific, commandments (slapping on the face is intimate and one on one; being insulted or cursed can be a collective affair).[47]

In verse 30 we read:

> Give to all that request of you; and from the one taking from you, do not demand it back.

43. Whitehead, "the Poetics of Violence," in Whitehead, *Violence*, 68–69.

44. Graeber, *Debt*, 103.

45. Graeber, *Debt*, 106.

46. Graeber, *Debt*, 193.

47. Marshall, *The Gospel of Luke*, 260.

Παντὶ αἰτοῦντί σε δίδου, καὶ ἀπὸ τοῦ αἴροντος τὰ σὰ μὴ ἀπαίτει.

Here are two commandments that end with the same result—the parting of ways with one's property—but which nevertheless start with two very different circumstances. With regards to the first commandment: to "give to all that request of you" (Παντὶ αἰτοῦντί σε δίδου), we find the same commandment, almost verbatim in the *Didache* (Παντὶ τῷ αἰτοῦντί σε) with the added phrasing "and do not demand it back" (καὶ μὴ ἀπαίτεν), echoing the second commandment in verse 30 of the Sermon (Didache 1.5). Further on, the *Didache* gives an explanation for the commandment:

> For the Father wants something from his own gifts to be given to everyone. (Didache 1.5)

It then goes on to clarify how the commandment works in practice (i.e. not asking for what you do not need and so on). Matthew also quotes the commandment in Matthew 5:42, but without direct clarification. The explanation in the *Didache* uses the logic of creation: God gives creation to mankind as a gift, and everyone should enjoy this gift; therefore, if someone asks for something, you should give; since in the end it belongs to God and he desires everyone to enjoy creation. It is a logical and appealing explanation, and one which was re-used throughout Church History.[48] This explanation however, is not found in the text of the Sermon on the Plain, the explanation in the Sermon comes later in verse 38; which has to do with, in my understanding, the formation of a certain kind of social relationship.

The picture presented in verse 30 is that of a beggar asking for alms and receiving a gift of mercy.[49] The idea of the "gift" is most famously theorized by the anthropologist Marcell Mauss, whose basic observation was:

> The most important feature among these spiritual mechanisms [of gift giving] is clearly one that obliges a person to reciprocate the present that has been received.[50]

In other words, there is a symbolic aspect of gift giving that requires the receiver to reciprocate, otherwise:

---

48. For example by Basil of Caesarea, and John Chrysostom, and many others.

49. Betz, *A commentary on the Sermon on the Mount, including the Sermon on the Plain*, 597–598.

50. Mauss, *The Gift*, 9.

The unreciprocated gift still makes the person who has accepted it inferior, particularly when it has been accepted with no thought of returning it.[51]

Marcell Mauss, in *The Gift*, argues that tribal societies engage in forms of reciprocity through gift giving; and that gift giving was an integral part of the tribal economic and spiritual structure. Jesus, in making the giving of gifts universally mandated, upends the general logic: gifts are freely given to anyone and everyone who asks. There can be a temptation to go the route of thinking that giving is, in some sense, a form of worship to God—in that it can be said to be a form of exchange which will be repaid by God. There is a logic of alms giving as reciprocal exchange with the divine in the Abrahamic tradition, on that topic Marcell Mauss writes:

> This is the ancient morality of the gift, which has become a prin-
> ciple of justice. The gods and the spirits accept that the share of
> wealth and happiness that has been offered to them and had been
> hitherto destroyed in useless sacrifices should serve the poor and
> children. In recounting this we are recounting the history of the
> moral ideas of the Semites. The Arab *sadaka* originally meant ex-
> clusively justice, as did the Hebrew *zedaqa*: it has come to mean
> alms. We can even date from the Mishnaic era, from the victory of
> the 'Poor' in Jerusalem, the time when the doctrine of charity and
> alms was born, which, with Christianity and Islam, spread around
> the world. It was at this time that the word *zedaqa* changed in
> meaning, because in the Bible it did not mean alms.[52]

Of course, in a sense this is true, the idea of giving to the poor being also a gift to God certainly does go back to the Hebrew bible.[53] However, as we will see later, this is not the logic of the Sermon; neither is this command-ment in the Sermon following the logic of a "gift economy." We know this because the giving commanded by Jesus is commanded universally, in that all (παντί) who ask are to be given to. As Marcell Mauss points out, gift giving generally requires discrimination:

> All these institutions [of reciprocal gift giving] express one fact
> alone, one social system, one precise state of mind: everything—
> food, women, children, property, talismans, land, labor services,
> priestly functions, and ranks—is there for passing on, and for

51. Mauss, *The Gift*, 83.

52. Mauss, *The Gift*, 23.

53. For example see Proverbs 11:24; 19:17; 28:27.

balancing accounts. Everything passes to and fro as if there were a constant exchange of a spiritual matter, including things and men, between clans and individuals, distributed between social ranks, the sexes, and the generations.[54]

The Gift economy is an entire network of customs and spiritual concepts that dictate how one should give and how one should reciprocate, Jesus overrides all of that. In doing so he makes equal reciprocity impossible; since giving to everyone will guarantee that many cannot reciprocate. He also overturns the logic of a reciprocal relationship with God through giving to the righteous; since giving to everyone will include those who are not righteous, deserving, or even in need. Perhaps they simply want to take advantage of the giver. The commandment does not allow for any consideration of the background of the beggar—why he is begging, or what he will use the gift for—to influence whether or not a gift is given.[55] Jesus's commandment overrides any connection between gift and legitimate claim, the command is simply unequivocal.[56] On the face of it the commandment seems absurd, which leads us to the second commandment in the verse.

The second example in verse 30 is, in a sense, the polar opposite: rather than a helpless beggar asking for alms, there is a powerful robber physically dispossessing you. There is no direct parallel to this commandment in the Sermon on the Mount. After the commandment to give, the Sermon on the Mount goes directly to the commandment to not refuse a borrower. The commandment is paralleled in the *Didache* however, but with an explanation:

> If someone takes from you what belongs to you, do not demand it back, for you cannot do so.
>
> . . .
>
> ἐὰν λάβῃ τις ἀπὸ σοῦ τὸ σόν, μὴ ἀπαίτει· οὐδὲ γὰρ δύνασαι. (Didache 1.4)

This adds a clarification: the assumption is that the one who steals from you is so powerful that demanding it back would be in vain, you cannot. This assumption however, is not in the Sermon on the Plain. In the Sermon, the victim is assumed to be in a position where there is a chance to get

---

54. Mauss, *The Gift*, 18.

55. Fitzmyer, *The Gospel According to Luke I–IX*, 639.

56. Marshall, *The Gospel of Luke*, 261.

back the goods; but he is commanded to forego that opportunity.[57] As we established above, violence is a way of stripping someone of his honor, and in Plato's Gorgias we read that one who lacks honor is one who can simply be stripped of his possessions, one who will not defend him or herself, one who can easily be dispossessed.

Jesus's instruction is to allow yourself to be stripped of your possessions and thus be rendered without honor. Again, the commandment is to not follow the social norms, neither the social norm of discriminate giving for some reciprocity; nor the social norm of violently establishing property rights and defending them. Given the context of a heavy burden of taxation, and the tendency for Galileans to resist this taxation and to resist the dispossession through credit instruments (as shown above), this commandment could also be read (anachronistically perhaps) as being anti-Zealot.[58] The most common form of dispossession that the average Galilean would experience would be from rent collectors, debt collectors, and tax collectors, and this would be backed by the ever present threat of violence, especially when it came to taxation.[59] Jesus here, in line with his general ethic of non-retaliation, would have been understood to be arguing against a Zealot style revolution.[60] This is ultimately intertwined with his ethic of generosity, both textually (in that in the Sermon the commandments go between generosity and non-resistance), as well as structurally in that ultimately both non-resistance and excessive generosity depend on trust in God.

Moving on to verse 31 we read the famous Golden Rule:

And just as YOU want people to do to YOU, YOU do likewise.

---

57. Betz, *A commentary on the Sermon on the Mount, including the Sermon on the Plain,* 598.

58. I use the term "Zealot" here loosely, to refer to the tendency in Galilee and Judea to violently resist Roman domination; not the proper sense of the word which refers to the revolutionary group active in Palestine in the 60s CE leading a Jewish revolt against Rome.

59. Simmons, "Taxation," in Barry, *The Lexham Bible Dictionary.*

60. The notion that the Sermon is teaching non-violence in a political sense is disputed, for example by Richard Horsley (Horsley, *Jesus and the Spiral of Violence,* 260–264; 267–268) on the basis that no actual political violence is ever mentioned in the context, and there is no evidence for a violent resistance movement at the time of Jesus. I however, do not think that political violence needs to be specifically mentioned to be included in a plausible interpretation; and even though there was no violent resistance movement at that time, there certainly was state violence from Rome and her collaborators, and there certainly was the memory of resistance (violent or otherwise) from the local populace.

Καὶ καθὼς θέλετε ἵνα ποιῶσιν ὑμῖν οἱ ἄνθρωποι ποιεῖτε αὐτοῖς ὁμοίως.

The parallel in the Sermon on the Mount gives us further clarification:

> "In everything do to others as you would have them do to you; for this is the law and the prophets. (Matt 7:12)

Here we have a formula which seems to have been part of Jewish oral tradition; in the Talmud we read an account of the rabbi Hillel meeting a gentile and converting him. The gentile had said he would convert to Judaism if the rabbi could tell him the entire Torah while he stood on one foot, Hillel replied:

> That which is hateful to you do not do to another; that is the entire Torah, and the rest is its interpretation. Go study. (Babylonian Talmud, *Sabbath*. 31a. [Steinsaltz Even-Yisrael])

Generally speaking "Q" theorists will say that Matthew interpolated the "for this is the law and the prophets"[61] in order to suit his Jewish audience.[62] Given that this formula may have already been in circulation as indicated by Hillel's rendition of the Golden rule, this is a possibility. Whatever the original version of Jesus's Golden rule (if we can even say that there is only one original version, Jesus may have rendered it differently at different times), we can say that Luke's rendition does not portray it as a summation of the moral principles of the Torah; although it is grounded in the commandment to love one's fellow found in Leviticus 19:18.[63] Another thing we can say is that Jesus's version is positive, whereas Hillel's is negative. Jesus commands to "do" (ποιεῖτε), whereas Hillel commands "do not do." The tradition in Judaism of the Golden rule is found further in Tobit (Tobit 4:15), Sirach (Sirach 31:15), Philo (Eusebius, *Praeparatio Evangelica*, 8.7), 2 Enoch (2 *Enoch* 61:2), and the Jerusalem Targum (*Tg. Ps.-J.*, Leviticus 19:18); and all those examples of the Golden rule are rendered as negative in nature.

The Golden rule was also common in Hellenistic moral thought; however, like Hillel's version, it was always negative. Three prominent examples are of Thales:

---

61. Kloppenborg, John, *Q the Earliest Gospel*, 126.

62. Betz, *A commentary on the Sermon on the Mount, including the Sermon on the Plain*, 599.

63. Allison, *Constructing Jesus*, 358–359.

How shall we lead the best and most righteous life?" "By refraining from doing what we blame in others." (Laertius, *Lives of the
Eminent Philosophers,* 1.36)

Isocrates:

Do not do to others that which angers you when they do it to you.
(Isocrates, *Nicocles or the Cyprians,* 3.61 [Norlin])

And Herodotus:

But what I condemn in another I will, if I may, avoid myself.
(Herodotus, *Histories,* 3.142 [Rawlinson])

We notice here that all three examples of the Golden rule are negative in nature: the point is to refrain from action that you would find objectionable.
The Hellenistic and Pharisaic concepts of the Golden rule are, in a sense,
precursors to the idea of negative freedoms—righteousness and virtue are
the result of refraining from harming others. Jesus's Golden rule is almost
the opposite—righteousness and virtue are the result of fulfilling your obligation to others: it is about action; non-action is not virtuous or righteous.

The negative version of the Golden rule, sometimes called the "Silver
Rule," was extremely common in both Jewish and Greco-Roman culture
around Jesus's time. What the Sermon on the Plain does is take this common
moral maxim and turn it on its head; taking a rule that usually legislated
against certain negative behavior, and making it legislate positive behavior
towards others. It turns a restriction on behavior into an obligation to act.

This commandment seems to differ from the previous block of commandments in the ethical portion of the Sermon. Verse 27 is the framework for what follows: it is an ethic of extreme counter-intuitive love that
casts aside self-interest and social norms. It is a love that manifests itself as
self-sacrificial in a near literal sense. The ethic of verse 31—though being
more radical than the negative freedom formulations common in the Jewish and Greco-Roman worlds—is not nearly as radical as the 27–30 ethic.
The Golden rule is measured, rational, and seemingly reciprocal; whereas
the previous verses completely overturn reciprocity. It has been suggested
that "do" (ποιεῖτε) should be read as an indicative rather than an imperative, in other words as describing the situation now as contrasted with how
Jesus wants his followers to act (laid out in verses 27–30, and 32–38).[64] This
interpretation is not at all necessary, nor is it very plausible; the Golden rule

---

64. Dihle, *Goldene Regel,* 113–114.

is connected with a "Καὶ" (and, or also), implying continuation with what preceded it. The Golden rule is not contrasted with verses 27–30, rather, it is continuous with them.[65]

A better interpretation is that Jesus moves from the extreme and radical self-sacrificial ethic of verses 27–30 to an accepted ethic of the Golden rule—with the added element of obligation. The framework for Jesus's Golden rule is not primarily the Hellenistic moral tradition but rather the Mosaic code found at Leviticus 19:18 which is obligatory in nature and—when taken as the framework for Jesus's Golden rule—ties the Golden rule with the beginning of the ethics section of the Sermon on the Plain in verse 27. The added element of obligation from the Mosaic Law is key here, and it lays the ground work for what follows. In the verses that follow, Jesus will show that in order to truly be faithful to the positive version of the commonly accepted "Golden rule" in verse 31—one must take on the radical self-sacrificial ethic of verses 27–30; and the verses that follow also show how that ethic actually works itself out. As we will see going forward, to follow the Golden rule correctly and faithfully, one must go much further than mere reciprocity—one must embrace the radical ethic of the rest of the Sermon.[66]

32–35

In verses 32–38 we have the "commandments"—which were laid out in the previous verses—explained and reasoned through. In verses 32–34a we have a series of rhetorical questions being asked. The intention of these questions is to challenge "common sense" or popular notions of social ethics:

> And if YOU love those loving YOU, what credit is it to YOU? For also the sinners love the ones loving them. [For] Also if YOU do good to those doing good to YOU, what credit is it to YOU? The sinners also do it. And if YOU lend to those from whom YOU hope to receive, what credit [is it] to YOU?

> καὶ εἰ ἀγαπᾶτε τοὺς ἀγαπῶντας ὑμᾶς, ποία ὑμῖν χάρις ἐστίν; καὶ γὰρ οἱ ἁμαρτωλοὶ τοὺς ἀγαπῶντας αὐτοὺς ἀγαπῶσιν.

---

65. Betz, *A commentary on the Sermon on the Mount, including the Sermon on the Plain*, 600.

66. Fitzmyer, *The Gospel According to Luke I–IX*, 639.

καὶ [γὰρ] ἐὰν ἀγαθοποιῆτε τοὺς ἀγαθοποιοῦντας ὑμᾶς, ποία ὑμῖν χάρις ἐστίν; καὶ οἱ ἁμαρτωλοὶ τὸ αὐτὸ ποιοῦσιν.

καὶ ἐὰν δανίσητε παρ' ὧν ἐλπίζετε λαβεῖν, ποία ὑμῖν χάρις [ἐστίν];

To love those who love you fits perfectly with traditional Hellenistic ethics where friendship is, at bottom, a form of exchange. The term used here for "credit" is χάρις, which is used in this context as the response, or the thanks, for generosity or benefaction.[67] The assumption behind this question is that "love" is akin to a gift: a gift which would warrant a response of gratitude.[68] Yet the point being made is that one would have to extend this "gift" of love beyond those who love you in return to warrant any credit, or gratitude. Jesus then goes on to say that "the sinners also do it." The parallel in Matthew puts it this way:

> or if you love those who love you, what reward (μισθὸν) do you have? Do not even the tax collectors do the same? And if you greet only your brothers and sisters, what more are you doing than others? Do not even the Gentiles do the same? (Matt 5:46–47)

In Luke, the term "sinners" is applied to unsavory types and it is usually used in conjunction with tax collectors (Luke 5:30; 7:34; 15:1–2), the rich,[69] as well as Gentiles in general (Luke 24:7). Looking at the parallel in Matthew, we can look back at verse 31 and say that the "people" (ἄνθρωποι)— with whom you are supposed to be practicing the Golden rule—are most probably Israelites; which places the ethical teaching of the Sermon in a Palestinian Jewish context.[70] Going back to the question of loving those who love you, we see that Matthew's version uses "reward" (μισθός) rather than Luke's "credit," or "thanks" (χάρις). The implication being that, for the Sermon on the Plain, the result of doing good is not any kind of quid pro quo; since χάρις, as opposed to μισθός, would not have the implication of a physical reward for good action, it would rather have the implication of receiving credit or thanks for it.[71] In the ancient world the idea of doing good to those who do good to you was common, and it fits perfectly with

---

67. BDAG, χάρις.

68. Betz, *A commentary on the Sermon on the Mount, including the Sermon on the Plain*, 600–601.

69. Crossley, *Why Christianity Happened*, 95.

70. Tuckett, *Q and the History of Early Christianity*, 431.

71. Evans, *Saint Luke*, 335.

mainstream ancient Hellenistic philosophy.[72] But for the Sermon, no χάρις can be expected from this kind of good work. As we saw in verse 27, love and good works go together, and love and good works are to be given to our enemies: those who hate us. In verse 32 an explanation of that commandment is hinted at: by doing good to your enemies and showing them love, you will receive χάρις. Those who treat love and good works in an exchange framework—where good works are meant to be reciprocal—are no better than the sinners who treat others as means to an end, who give to those who can return the benefit in some fashion.

The third question brings in a new concept: lending. This is a switch from a general principle to a specific example of that principle being applied in practice. To fully understand the specific question in verse 34; let us take it along with its answer in verse 35:

> And if YOU lend to those from whom YOU hope to receive, what credit [is it] to YOU? Sinners also lend to sinners in order that they might get back the same. Nevertheless, love YOUR enemies, and do good and lend expecting nothing in return, and YOUR reward will be great, and YOU will be sons of the Most High—because he is gracious upon the ungrateful and wicked.

> καὶ ἐὰν δανίσητε παρ' ὧν ἐλπίζετε λαβεῖν, ποία ὑμῖν χάρις [ἐστίν]; καὶ ἁμαρτωλοὶ ἁμαρτωλοῖς δανίζουσιν ἵνα ἀπολάβωσιν τὰ ἴσα.

> πλὴν ἀγαπᾶτε τοὺς ἐχθροὺς ὑμῶν καὶ ἀγαθοποιεῖτε καὶ δανίζετε μηδὲν ἀπελπίζοντες· καὶ ἔσται ὁ μισθὸς ὑμῶν πολύς, καὶ ἔσεσθε υἱοὶ ὑψίστου, ὅτι αὐτὸς χρηστός ἐστιν ἐπὶ τοὺς ἀχαρίστους καὶ πονηρούς.

In this specific application of Jesus's ethical principles, we have an issue dealt with in the Mosaic Law, an issue well discussed by the pharisaic rabbis: lending, and return on loans. In the Mosaic code, lending on interest was strictly forbidden (Exod 22:25; Lev 25:36–37; Deut 23:19–20), but what that actually meant in practice was subject to interpretation. The main thrust of the pharisaic interpretation of the usury laws was that the point of the law was that any loan was not to profit the creditor—even unintentionally. Whatever was lent was to be returned with the same value, no more no less. To illustrate this interpretation, we can read rabbi Hillel's ruling on the lending of bread:

---

72. Marshall, *The Gospel of Luke*, 262.

A woman may not lend a loaf of bread to her neighbor unless she determines its value in money, lest wheat should rise in price and they be found partakers in usury. (Mishnah, *Baba Metzia*. 5.9)

The idea here is that all lending should be an equal exchange, one amount lent out to the borrower and the same amount returned to the lender; this would require that exact measurements and pricing should take place to ensure the equal value of what is given in the loan and what is returned. The beginning of this discussion in the Mishnah starts with the usury laws as recorded in Leviticus 25:36–37, where the focus is on not charging interest or receiving an increase (or profit) from one's fellow Israelite (Mishnah, *Baba Metzia*. 5.1). Jesus on the other hand goes much further, he says no return is to be expected at all. The use of τὰ ἴσα in verse 34 makes it clear that Jesus is not just talking about a return on investment—a profit—but rather the return of any of the principle, thus making any measurement of value pointless.[73]

Marshall Howard argues in his commentary on Luke that the return refers not to a return on the principle; but rather to an expectation of a reciprocal loan in the future. His argument is that "sinners" do not lend to regain the principle, but to make a profit; therefore the "return" could not be regaining the principle, but it is more likely to be a return in the form of a future loan.[74] The problem with this interpretation is that lenders who profit from interest are engaging in business—not the giving of loans to build relationships which they can later appeal to for mutual aid—so, "sinners" making these loans usually are not expecting loans from their creditors if they are charging interest. A better interpretation is that these sinners (or perhaps Gentiles)[75] are expecting at least the principle back—whether these loans are of a business nature or are more informal—Gentiles do not want to be taken advantage of and therefore will expect at least the principle back, requiring an initial valuation of the loan. Further validation of this

73. Betz, *A commentary on the Sermon on the Mount, including the Sermon on the Plain*, 603–604.

74. Marshall, *The Gospel of Luke*, 263.

75. The idea that "sinners" refers to Gentiles is disputed by Richard Horsley (Horsley, *Jesus and the Spiral of Violence*, 268–269) on the basis that it would have referred to people that the audience would be familiar with. Although I do not think we can say either way whether it refers to Gentiles or unsavoury types within the Jewish community, there is no reason to assume that the members of the audience of the Sermon were not familiar with non-Jewish lending practices.

interpretation can be found in the rendering of this commandment in the Gospel of Thomas:

> [Jesus said], "If you have money, don't lend it at interest. Rather, give [it] to someone from whom you won't get it back." (Gospel of Thomas 95 [Patterson and Meyer])

From this rendition of the commandment we learn that the commandment was related to the anti-usury laws, and that the return was the return of the actual money, not a favor or a reciprocal loan.

Some have argued that Jesus's commandment to expect nothing in return is, in effect, turning the loan into a gift: a free act of benevolence that mirrors divine benevolence.[76] The problem with this view is that the text makes it clear that it is a loan being spoken of in verses 34–35; it never switches to being a gift. Verse 30 deals with gifts, making it a separate category and a separate commandment. Given this, it is clear that we are still in the realm of lending, the handing over of goods which explicitly includes a mutual obligation assigned to the borrower.

The difference between a gift and a debt obligation and between their implications is significant. The giving of gifts, in the Greco-Roman world, was a large part of the institution of benefaction (or patronage); which, as we discussed earlier, was a hierarchical relationship in which the wealthier party would exchange material goods for the honor and loyalty of the poorer party. In this situation the "gift" is not an act of sharing implying a mutual obligation and a recognition of one's dependence on his fellow; but rather it implies superiority on one end, and inferiority on the other. David Graeber puts it this way:

> "Gift" here does not mean something given freely, not mutual aid that we can ordinarily expect human beings to provide to one another. To thank someone [accepting something as a gift that is] suggests that he or she might not have acted that way, and therefore the choice to act that way creates an obligation, as sense of debt—and hence, inferiority.[77]

In this kind of gift giving situation, one is not "lending" to another in the sense of an explicitly agreed upon exchange, nor is one giving or lending in the sense of sharing; but rather, one is practicing benefaction, in which

---

76. Garland, *Exegetical Commentary on the New Testament: Luke*, 486–487; Betz, *A commentary on the Sermon on the Mount, including the Sermon on the Plain*, 607–609.

77. Graeber, *Debt*, 116.

the giver displays his superiority by giving a gift to the inferior, who is expected to recognize the givers superiority. In many societies—especially honor-based hierarchical societies—games of gift giving and counter gift giving could end up in the extreme, as each party tries to outdo the other so as to establish his superiority.[78] This was the case in the first-century Mediterranean world where games of honor could include violence (such as slapping someone on the face) or non-violent challenges in the form of extravagant gift giving meant to diminish the receiver's social position.[79] In these games the relative value of the gift was extremely important.[80] This was the case in the institution of benefaction, where a patron's honor was heavily affected by the size and prominence of a his clientele, which depended on how much he could provide in benefaction.[81] Of course, not all gift giving was done within the context of patron-client relationships; it was also a factor in Hellenistic concepts of friendship. For example, Aristotle, in speaking on gifts between friends, distinguishes between friendships based on utility—where gifts are given in order to get a repayment, and valued for their utility, and the utility of the repayment—and friendships based on virtue—where gifts are given for the sake of virtue and valued simply because of the virtue of the giver (Aristotle, *Ethics*, 8.13). However, as we discussed earlier, these kinds of friendships depended on an equality of status; if the status of the individuals changed, the friendship would be more or less impossible and it would dissolve, or it would turn into a relationship of benefaction (Aristotle, *Ethics*, 8.14).

Lending, on the other hand, has different implications. However, a crucial distinction within the realm of lending needs to be made: between calculated lending and uncalculated lending. David Graeber puts the difference this way:

> The difference between a debt and an obligation is that a debt can be precisely quantified.[82]

Calculated lending results in a quantified debt; whereas uncalculated lending results in a mutual obligation. In describing an attitude of an Inuit

78. Graeber, *Debt*, 105–106.

79. Malina, *The New Testament World*, 33.

80. Graeber, *Toward and Anthropological Theory of Value*, 221–222.

81. Kalinowski, "Patterns of Patronage," 11–12.

82. Graeber, *Debt*, 21.

hunter, an attitude found often among hunter gatherer-societies, David Graeber writes:

> Rather than seeing himself as human because he could make economic calculations, the hunter insisted that being truly human meant refusing to make such calculations, refusing to measure or remember who had given what to whom, for the precise reason that doing so would inevitably create a world where we began "comparing power with power, measuring, calculative" and reducing each other to slaves or dogs through debt.[83]

Interestingly, the attitude that Graeber is describing in the Inuit hunter comes from that hunter's response to being thanked by a Danish writer for giving him meat from a hunt. The idea being that by accepting thanks the hunter is acknowledging that he was not obligated to share his meat and that by receiving the meat given, the Danish writer is placed in an inferior position.[84] The actual quote from the Inuit responding to the writer is:

> "Up in our country we are human" said the hunter. "And since we are human we help each other. We don't like to hear anybody say thanks for that. What I get today you may get tomorrow. Up here we say that by gifts one makes slaves and by whips one makes dogs."[85]

This hunter's idea about gifts agrees with the Hellenistic concept of benefaction: it creates a hierarchy and puts one as the more honorable superior over the subservient inferior party. Moving back to calculated debts verses uncalculated obligations Graeber says:

> The difference between owing someone a favor, and owing someone a debt, is that the amount of a debt can be precisely calculated. Calculation demands equivalence And such equivalence—especially when it involves equivalence between human beings (and it always seems to start that way, because at first, human beings are always the ultimate values)—only seems to occur when people have been forcibly severed from their contexts, so much so that they can be treated as identical to something else, as in: "seven martin skins and twelve large silver rings for the return of your

---

83. Graeber, *Debt*, 79.

84. Graeber, *Debt*, 79.

85. Freuchen, *Book of the Eskimos*, 154.

captured brother," "one of your three daughters as a surety for this loan of one hundred and fifty bushels of grain" . . .[86]

This is crucial, within families, friends, and among almost all non-state tribal societies, people do not so much trade goods and services, as much as they build up networks of mutual obligations, mutual aid, and loosely owe each other favors. Another word for this is "communism"[87] in the anthropological/sociological sense.[88] When violence is introduced however, the trust necessary for communism, or uncalculated mutual obligations, goes away. In such a situation calculation must come into the picture and networks of mutual obligations must be replaced with exchange,[89] where each party merely contracts himself into relationship with the assumption that the other will try to take advantage of him.[90]

This brings us back to the Inuit hunter, he made sure that his sharing of meat was done within a communistic context: it was just sharing with the understanding that people would share with him; and not some kind of debt in which the receiver would have to repay a specific amount, nor a kind of benefaction in which the receiver would be seen as inferior. In other words, the Inuit hunter was making it clear that the relationship was one of trust, not one in which the parties were willing to use violence. This is the difference between a calculated debt and an uncalculated obligation— the uncalculated obligation assumes trust; the calculated debt assumes the probability of violence.

In order to make sense of Jesus's understanding of the usury laws and what the implications of those laws were for his moral view on lending we should look back to the concept of the Jubilee/Sabbatical year. In verses

86. Graeber, *Debt*, 386.

87. I use the term "communism" in this book to refer to the sociological/anthropological phenomenon in which individuals relate to each other under the general presumption of "from each according to his ability to each according to his need;" not the political sense of the term. This can apply to anything from two friends working on a common project, to an entire village economy, to a monastery, or even the idea behind social insurance systems. "Communism" in this sense is a moral framework for relationships based on mutual obligations; in other words, uncalculated debt.

88. Graeber, *Debt*, 98–100.

89. I use the term "exchange" to refer to the sociological/anthropological phenomenon in which individuals relate to each other under the general presumption of "tit for tat," or "quid pro quo." This applies to everything from gift exchange, to market sales and purchases, to contractual debt obligations and so on; the moral framework being that of contractual equivalence of exchange, requiring calculation.

90. Graeber, *Debt*, 213.

34–35 the word for lend is δανίζω, this word is used in the LXX version of the Sabbatical year legislation in Deuteronomy 15, which itself is the background to the Jubilee law in Leviticus 25[91] (which is also the chapter in Leviticus dealing with usury). The connection between Luke 6:34–35 and Deuteronomy 15 with regards their use of the term δανίζω is specifically found in Deuteronomy 15:8:[92]

> By opening, you shall open your hands to him; you shall lend a loan (δάνειον δανιεῖς) to him whatever he may need, in accord with what he needs.

The allusion to Deuteronomy 15 in the Sermon helps to explain the logic Jesus is using. Deuteronomy 15:1–2 explains the Sabbatical year law: every seven years there is to be a release (ἀφίημι) of debts, they are not to ask for what is owed back; in the third verse it makes it clear that this law applies to loans given to fellow Israelites, not foreigners. In verses 4–6 we have an explanation of the law—so that there will be no one in (ἐνδεής) need among them—which is guaranteed by God's blessing. In the first four verses of Deuteronomy 15 we have a regular release mechanism in place at regular intervals of seven years which exists for the sake of the social welfare of the poor. In verses 5–6 there is a promise that if the commandment is followed the result would be God's blessing and prosperity.

Verses 7–9 anticipate some pushback on the law and therefore commands that one is obligated to lend to the needy, even if the Sabbatical year is close and the loan will be released. It is in verse 8 that we get the command to:

> Lend a loan to him whatever he may need, in accord with what he needs.
>
> δάνειον δανιεῖς αὐτῷ ὅσον ἐπιδέεται, καθ᾽ ὅσον ἐνδεῖται.

In verse 10 we have a combination of "give" (δίδωμι) being used along with "lend" (δανίζω):

> Giving you shall give to him (διδοὺς δώσεις αὐτῷ), and you shall lend him a loan whatever he needs (καὶ δάνειον δανιεῖς αὐτῷ ὅσον ἐπιδέεται), and you shall not be grieved in your heart when you

---

91. Tuckett, *Q and the History of Early Christianity*, 430.

92. The LXX versions of the usury laws in Leviticus 25:36–37; Deuteronomy 23:19–20 do not use δανίζω. Exodus 22:25 uses a form of δανίζω, but it is only in Deuteronomy 15 that the same form of δανίζω as the form used in the Sermon is used.

give to him, because through this thing the Lord your God will bless you in all your works and in all to which you may put your hand.

The distinction is important in interpreting the Sermon, because we see that giving and lending are two different actions. Giving includes no explicit obligation of return (although there often is an implicit obligation); lending on the other hand, includes an obligation—sometimes legal, sometimes informal—of return, however, this obligation is mediated by anti-usury laws and the Sabbatical year release law. In Deuteronomy 15, lending is an economic mechanism whose purpose is social welfare; whereas giving is commanded but clearly distinguished from lending, as it is in the Sermon.

Moving back to the Sermon on the Plain we see this logic play out in Jesus's commandments. If one is expecting the release of debts, there would be no reason to calculate what is owed—since soon the debts will be released anyway. Yet, the clear command in Deuteronomy as well as in Jesus's sermon is to lend anyway; in Deuteronomy, to lend according to the receiver's need. What results from the Sabbatical year, which essentially eliminates the need to calculate loans, is that calculated debts functioning on the "exchange ethic" turn into uncalculated obligations functioning on the "communist ethic."

Rabbi Hillel's interpretation of the anti-usury laws is that of extreme commodification: everything must be priced, down to the bread one loans to a neighbor, in order to avoid committing usury. The assumption of Hillel is that of an exchange ethic, as would apply to business loans, or market exchanges. For Hillel, the usury laws are meant to avoid economic exploitation, therefore, we need to price everything so that no one gets exploited through the credit system. This is likely because Rabbi Hillel seems to be looking at usury only through the law as found at Leviticus 25. Jesus's interpretation is to view the anti-usury laws through the light of the Sabbatical year law in Deuteronomy 15; which makes loans more about building communities of mutual aid rather than just making sure exchanges are equal and non-exploitative.

Rabbi Hillel does, in a different tractate, comment on the anti-usury and Sabbatical law found in Deuteronomy 15:

> This is one of the things that Hillel the Elder ordained. When he says that the people refrained from giving loans one to another and transgressed what is written in the Law, *Beware that there be*

not a base thought in thine heart . . ., Hillel ordained the *prozbul*.
prozbul.[93]

This is the formula of the *prozbul*: 'I affirm to you, such-a-
one and such-a-one, the judges in such-a-place, that, touching
any debt due to me, I will collect it when-so-ever I will. (Mishnah,
Shebiith. 10.3–4)

Later on, in the tractate it makes clear that the rabbis encourage the debtor
to repay the debt even if the creditor fails to collect the loan (Mishnah,
Shebiith. 10.9). Here we again see Hillel treating lending as primarily an
exchange arrangement. The release of the Sabbatical law, which Jesus in
the Sermon used as a framework for turning loans into a mechanism that
would create a "communist" ethic of mutual aid, Hillel sees as a hindrance
to be overcome. Once again, Hillel is assuming an exchange ethic in the
community, and rather than try to change that ethic he attempts to re-
interpret the law to fit it; even to the point of creating the *prozbul*, which
basically undoes the point of the law completely. Hillel's *prozbul* would
make debt a perpetual burden.[94]

We get a similar opinion to the Sermon's position on lending, although
slightly different and more detailed in Sirach 29:

Many regard a loan as a windfall (πολλοὶ ὡς εὕρεμα ἐνόμισαν δάνος),
and they caused trouble for those who helped them. Until he receives it he will kiss his hands, and about his fellow's money (τῶν
χρημάτων τοῦ πλησίον) he lowers his voice, and at the moment
for repayment he will delay for a time and will pay back words of
apathy, and he will blame the time. If he is capable he will recover
scarcely half, and he will consider that as a windfall (καὶ λογιεῖται
αὐτὸ ὡς εὕρεμα); but if not, he has defrauded him of his money,
and he has needlessly made him an enemy (καὶ ἐκτήσατο αὐτὸν
ἐχθρὸν δωρεάν); curses and insults he will repay him, and instead
of glory he will repay him dishonor (καὶ ἀντὶ δόξης ἀποδώσει
αὐτῷ ἀτιμίαν). Many turned away not because of wickedness;
they were wary of being defrauded needlessly. Nevertheless, with
a lowly person be patient, and do not make him wait for charity
(ἐλεημοσύνη). On account of the commandment, assist a needy
person, and according to his need (κατὰ τὴν ἔνδειαν αὐτοῦ) do not
turn him away empty. Lose silver for the sake of a brother and a

93. The word *prozbul* likely comes from a Greek word *prosbole*, which one can find in
juristic documents referring to the taking of property of a defaulting debtor and auction-
ing it. Oakman, *Jesus and the Peasants*, 17.

94. Oakman, *Jesus and the Peasants*, 188.

friend, and do not let it corrode under the stone into destruction. Dispose of your treasure according to the commandment of the Most High, and it will profit you more than gold. Store up charity (ἐλεημοσύνην) in your treasuries, and it will deliver you from every affliction. (Sirach 29:4–12)

Sirach, in the second part of this passage, tells the lender to—even in the face of a potential loss—lend anyway "on account of the commandment" (almost certainly the commandment in Deuteronomy 15), and to do so "according to his need." Sirach, like Jesus, takes this extremely seriously, hinting at the idea that to not do so would lead to one's destruction; but by doing so one will profit "more than gold" from the Most High.

The first part of this passage addresses the borrower and complains that many regard a loan as a "windfall" (εὕρεμα), or a piece of good luck. This unrighteous borrower manipulates the lender to get a loan from him and then does not pay it back, turning what was once a "fellow" (πλησίον) into an enemy (ἐχθρὸν). Sirach then betrays his Hellenistic/Roman "benefaction"/"patronage" thinking when he says, "instead of glory he will repay him dishonor." Sirach thought of lending to the poor, showing "charity" (ἐλεημοσύνην), as part of an exchange for "glory" (δόξης).

This is different from the logic of the Sabbatical year commandment and the Jubilee commandment—where the debts were going to be cancelled anyway, and the land redistributed[95]—and where the lending was meant to maintain economic equality and security in the land. In this sense, the Sermon on the Plain is remaining faithful to the idea behind the Sabbatical year law; in that it commands that one should lend, not expecting a return, and not being bothered if no return came; but rather one should not expect anything in return on account of one's respecting the Sabbatical year release.

The Blessings and woes in verses 20–26, the eschatological reversal, gives us a hint that the ethics—including the ethics of lending—have in mind the reversals of the Jubilee and the Sabbatical laws. The Sermon's connection between the eschatological reversal and the ethics of lending helps to make sense of the seemingly paradoxical commandment; and it helps explain the Sermon's differences with both Hillel and Sirach. Since the eschatological reversal modeled on the Jubilee/Sabbatical release was there in the beginning of the Sermon, it makes perfect sense that similar themes run through the ethics; and it makes perfect sense that the Jubilee/

95. In the Jubilee law of Leviticus 25.

Sabbatical release ought to be our primary exegetical framework for at least the economic portions of the Sermon.

36–38

Verse 36 brings in the notion of mercy:

> Become merciful just as YOUR father is [also] merciful to YOU.

> Γίνεσθε οἰκτίρμονες καθὼς [καὶ] ὁ πατὴρ ὑμῶν οἰκτίρμων ἐστίν.

and ties it with a commandment to imitate God in that regard. This follows from verse 35 in that God's mercy was often seen in terms of how he materially provides for his people.[96] This idea—that of God being the model of mercy for his servants to imitate—was common in both Jewish and Early Christian thinking,[97] and the term merciful (οἰκτίρμων) was used frequently in conjunction with God in the LXX.[98] In the ancient Hellenistic world in general, mercy was not thought of as necessarily a good trait, being associated with emotion rather than reason. According to the general way of thinking in the Hellenistic world, a virtuous man would not be swayed by weak emotions such as mercy but would rather stick to reason.[99]

Seneca's work *On Clemency* gives us a window into the standard Greco-Roman view of mercy, through the stoic eyes of Seneca. Seneca conceives of clemency as the trait of a sovereign power: one who has the power of life and death over others (Seneca, *On Clemency 1, 19*). Violence can be done by anyone to anyone; but only a powerful sovereign can show clemency, because there is no need for him to establish, or demonstrate, his superiority through violence; since his superiority is already evident. Therefore, showing clemency can be a good way to actually demonstrate power and superiority, in a rather calculated way (Seneca, *On Clemency 1, 21*). Seneca's analysis of clemency is very hierarchical in nature: one shows clemency or mercy on the lower classes because of one's high position and

---

96. Psalms 29(30):11(10); 102(103):4–6; 110(111):4–5; 143(144):2 in the LXX.

97. Marshall, *The Gospel of Luke*, 265; Betz, *A commentary on the Sermon on the Mount, including the Sermon on the Plain*, 613. One striking parallel is found in Ephesians 5:1: "Therefore be imitators of God, as beloved children." This not only calls to mind Luke 6:36, but also the previous verse 35, which promises that those who follow Jesus's commandments will be "sons of the "Most High."

98. Evans, *Saint Luke*, 337.

99. Stark, *The Triumph of Christianity*, 112.

virtue, and by doing so one increases his honor (Seneca, *On Clemency 1,*
17–18). Seneca also appeals to divinities in his discussion of clemency, but
he makes sure to follow the standard stoic view: we are to be rational and in
line with the natural order:

> Fierce and implacable rage does not befit a king, because he does
> not preserve his superiority over the man to whose level he de-
> scends by indulging in rage; but if he grants their lives and honors
> to those who are in jeopardy and who deserve to lose them, he
> does what can only be done by an absolute ruler; for life may be
> torn away even from those who are above us in station, but can
> never be granted save to those who are below us. To save men's
> lives is the privilege of the loftiest station, which never deserves
> admiration so much as when it is able to act like the gods, by
> whose kindness good and bad men alike are brought into the
> world. Thus a prince, imitating the mind of a god, ought to look
> with pleasure on some of his countrymen because they are useful
> and good men, while he ought to allow others to remain to fill up
> the roll; he ought to be pleased with the existence of the former,
> and to endure that of the latter. (Seneca, *On Clemency 1, 5*)

The idea here is that the gods use virtuous men for their purposes, and they
tolerate the existence of others; therefore, a ruler—who has, in a sense, the
power of a god—ought to also tolerate the less than virtuous. Here, imitat-
ing the gods is described as tolerating un-virtue—where one would have the
power to punish un-virtue—and by doing so displaying one's superiority.

Both cruelty and pity are condemned by Seneca because they are not
driven by reason in line with the natural order and because they are the
result of a weak mind that is moved by emotion rather than reason. Seneca
says:

> Pity considers a man's misfortunes and does not consider to what
> they are due: mercy is combined with reason.
>
> . . .
>
> Pity is a disorder of the mind caused by the sight of other
> men's miseries, or it is a sadness caused by the evils with which
> it believes others to be undeservedly afflicted: but the wise man
> cannot be affected by any disorder: his mind is calm, and noth-
> ing can possibly happen to ruffle it. Moreover, nothing becomes
> a man more than magnanimity: but magnanimity cannot coexist
> with sorrow. (Seneca, *On Clemency 2, 5*)

As opposed to pity, clemency or mercy is not emotion driven; it is reason driven, looking out for the maintaining of proper order, not mere sentimental relief for the weak. Seneca goes on to say:

> He will not show or feel any disgust at a man's having withered legs, or a flabby wrinkled skin, or supporting his aged body upon a staff; but he will do good to those who deserve it, and will, like a god, look benignantly upon all who are in trouble. Pity borders upon misery: it is partly composed of it and partly derived from it. You know that eyes must be weak, if they fill with rheum at the sight of another's blearedness, just as it is not real merriment but hysteria which makes people laugh because others laugh, and yawn whenever others open their jaws: pity is a defect in the mind of people who are extraordinarily affected by suffering, and he who requires a wise man to exhibit it is not far from requiring him to lament and groan when strangers are buried. (Seneca, *On Clemency 2, 6*)

In the end, Seneca clarifies his position: what ought to be punished must be punished, and what ought not to be punished cannot be punished. Clemency, for Seneca, is ultimately simply about doing what reason requires, but also making sure everything is taken into account. No one who ought to be punished can ever be allowed to escape punishment. One can wonder at this point if we are actually speaking of mercy at all, or if we are speaking of a mere utilitarian notion of justice (Seneca, *On Clemency 2, 7*).

This is in contrast to the Judaic view of God's mercy (and according to the Sermon on the Plain, the mercy we ought to imitate). In the Jewish tradition, God's mercy was not a display of power, nor did it fulfil a utilitarian purpose; rather, it was an honoring of the covenant God had with his people. In Psalms 110(111):4–5 we read:

> He made mention of his wonderful deeds; merciful and compassionate (ἐλεήμων καὶ οἰκτίρμων) is the Lord. Food he provided for those who fear him; he will be ever mindful of his covenant.

And in Psalms 88(89):2(1)–5(4) we read:

> Of your mercies, O Lord, I will sing forever; to generation and generation I will proclaim your truth with my mouth, because you said, "Forever mercy will be built (Εἰς τὸν αἰῶνα ἔλεος οἰκοδομηθήσεται)." In the heavens your truth will be prepared. I made a covenant with my chosen ones; I swore to David my slave:

'Forever I will provide offspring for you and will build your throne for generation and generation.'"

This changes the concept of mercy from a benefaction of a superior given to an inferior, to a covenantal obligation: God shows mercy, not to gain anything from his people, not to assert his power; but to be faithful to the covenant, the promise, he made to them. We also notice that mercy and compassion are taken together (ἐλεήμων καὶ οἰκτίρμων);[100] so this is not merely a cold rational decision, or a duty, but it is also driven by love and compassion. Much like the acts of kindness within a marriage, or the service a soldier does for his country, God's mercy is both a covenantal obligation and also driven by love. The logic of imitation in the Sermon with regards mercy is likely derived from Leviticus where it says:

> Speak to the congregation of the sons of Israel, and you shall say to them: You shall be holy ("Αγιοι ἔσεσθε), for I am holy, the Lord your God. (Lev 19:2, also repeated in 20:26)

Both verse 36 of the Sermon and the LXX translation of Leviticus have an ethical attribute commanded in the second person plural (ἔσεσθε in Leviticus, Γίνεσθε in the Sermon), followed by the explanation of that commandment being that it is an attribute of God.[101] This points us to the idea that the Sermon is drawing from the LXX in its command to be merciful.

As we mentioned earlier, mercy, in the biblical tradition, involves positive action—providing aid for those in need—and it is also tied with lending. Psalm 36(37):26, speaking about a righteous man, says:

> All day long he is merciful and lends (ὅλην τὴν ἡμέραν ἐλεᾷ καὶ δανείζει), and his offspring shall become a blessing.

Psalm 111(112):4–5 also says (again, about the righteous man):

> In darkness light dawned for the upright ones; merciful and compassionate and righteous (ἐλεήμων καὶ οἰκτίρμων καὶ δίκαιος) is he. Kind is the man who is compassionate and lends (χρηστὸς ἀνὴρ ὁ οἰκτίρων καὶ κιχρῶν); he will manage his words with discretion.

This links mercy with what is to come, and it also links it with what we have already read in verses 34–35 of the Sermon dealing with the commandment to lend. In Sirach 29:1–2 we get a similar connection:

100. See also Psalms 39(40):12(11); 50(51):3(1); 68(69):17(16); 76(77):9(8)–10(9); 85(86):15; 102(103):4, 8; 111(112):4; 144(145):8; Sirach 2:11 in the LXX.

101. Allison, *Constructing Jesus*, 355–356.

He who does mercy will lend to his fellow ('Ο ποιῶν ἔλεος δανιεῖ τῷ πλησίον), and he who prevails with his hand keeps the commandments. Lend to your fellow in his time of need (δάνεισον τῷ πλησίον ἐν καιρῷ χρείας αὐτοῦ), and again pay back your fellow at the proper time.

This passage gives us a little bit of the logic of why mercy and lending are tied together. Lending is a way to keep the commandment in Deuteronomy 15; however, it requires one to show mercy in the biblical sense: showing faithfulness to a covenant by aiding those in need. Just in the same way God is faithful to his covenant by providing aid when his people need it; the Israelites are to show mercy and follow the commandment to lend to those in need.

Looking at the commandment to "become merciful just as YOUR father is [also] merciful to YOU" through the lens of the Jewish tradition—such as what we find in the LXX translation of the Hebrew Bible and other Jewish literature; rather than the Hellenistic philosophical tradition—puts the commandment in conversation with the previous verses and those that follow in the Sermon. It is not that the audience of the Sermon are in positions of power and are being told to show clemency to those on whom they can justifiably inflict violence so as to maintain the natural order; rather, they are to be faithful to the covenant, as their heavenly father is, showing mercy to their fellow in their time of need as they are commanded to do.

Moving to verses 37–38 we read:

Also do not judge, and YOU will not be judged; and do not condemn, and YOU will not be condemned; release, and YOU will be released, give, and it will be given to YOU, they will give a good measure, pressed down, shaken, overflowing in YOUR bosom—for that measure YOU measure out, it will be measured in return to YOU.

Καὶ μὴ κρίνετε, καὶ οὐ μὴ κριθῆτε· καὶ μὴ καταδικάζετε, καὶ οὐ μὴ καταδικασθῆτε. ἀπολύετε, καὶ ἀπολυθήσεσθε· δίδοτε, καὶ δοθήσεται ὑμῖν· μέτρον καλὸν πεπιεσμένον σεσαλευμένον ὑπερεκχυννόμενον δώσουσιν εἰς τὸν κόλπον ὑμῶν· ᾧ γὰρ μέτρῳ μετρεῖτε ἀντιμετρηθήσεται ὑμῖν.

Here we get a four-fold exhortation: do not judge, do not condemn, release, and give. The command to not judge and not condemn go together in this context, judging and condemning here refer roughly to similar concepts: to refrain from showing mercy, to show an attitude of censoriousness, or to otherwise condemn.[102] Like the commandment to be merciful, the commandment to refrain from judging also seems to have its roots in Leviticus 19:

> You shall not do something unjust in judgment; you shall not accept the person of the poor or admire the person of a high official; with justice you shall judge your neighbor (ἐν δικαιοσύνῃ κρινεῖς τὸν πλησίον σου). (Lev 19:15)

And slightly later:

> You shall not hate in your mind your kin; in reproof you shall reprove your neighbor, and you shall not assume guilt because of him. (Lev 19:17)

In a similar way to what he does in verse 27 of the Sermon with Leviticus 19:18, in verse 37 Jesus is inverting a Levitical commandment to make it more extreme.[103]

As we will see later however, in one of the parables, this judgment/condemnation should not be limited to personal judgment or condemnation (as some commentators tend to do).[104] What is being referred to here would also include judgments and condemnations from an official, or a judicial source, which gives this commandment somewhat revolutionary implications. The "and YOU will not be judged/condemned" phrase could be thought of in terms of the Golden rule, in which the person who will not be doing the judging or condemning is a fellow human. It could also be read as an eschatological statement, in which by not judging and condemning you will avoid judgment and condemnation from God in the *eschaton*. The eschatological interpretation of the καὶ οὐ μὴ (and you will not be) statements is given further support by verse 35, in which one reward for following the correct course is:

> and YOUR reward will be great, and YOU will be sons of the Most High—because he is gracious upon the ungrateful and wicked.

Thus, we have a precedent for interpreting the outcome of good behavior in an eschatological way.[105] More precedent is given if we look at a Pauline parallel in Romans:

---

102. Marshall, *The Gospel of Luke*, 265.

103. Allison, *Constructing Jesus*, 357–358.

104. For example, Fitzmyer, *The Gospel According to Luke I–IX*, 641.

105. Betz, *A commentary on the Sermon on the Mount, including the Sermon on the*

> Why do you pass judgment on your brother or sister? Or you, why
> do you despise your brother or sister? For we will all stand before
> the judgment seat of God. (Rom 14:10)

Here we have a condemnation of judgement on the basis that we will be
judged, by God, in the *eschaton*. Another parallel in favor of an eschatological interpretation is found in Ephesians:

> and be kind to one another, tenderhearted, forgiving (χαριζόμενοι)
> one another, as God in Christ has forgiven (ἐχαρίσατο) you. (Eph
> 4:32)

Here, the logic for forgiving one another is that God has forgiven us. It
is significant that χαρίζομαι is used here rather than ἀπολύετε, since the
former (at least in the context of Ephesians 4:32) has more of a connotation
of pardoning wrongdoing.[106]

There is good evidence for both interpretations and, as we have seen
and will see, there is often room for more than one interpretation to be true
at the same time. A perhaps preferable interpretation would be to include
both: The Sermon is teaching moral behavior that will build a cohesive and
well-functioning community; as well as moral behavior that will result in
Divine favor in the *eschaton*.

Before moving on to examine the term "release" (ἀπολύετε), I would
like to look at two parallels from late first-century or early second-century
Christian literature found in 1 Clement and Polycarp's letter to the Philippians. The parallel in 1 Clement says:

> For he spoke as follows: "Show mercy, that you may be shown
> mercy; forgive, that it may be forgiven you; as you do so will it be
> done to you; as you give so will it be given to you; as you judge so
> will you be judged; as you are kind so will kindness be shown to
> you; with which measure you measure with, it will be measured to
> you." (1 Clement 13.2 [Holmes])

And the one in Polycarp (which you may remember from the analysis of
the blessings and woes given above) says:

> But remembering what the Lord said when he taught: Do not
> judge so that you may not be judged, forgive and then you will
> be forgiven; show mercy and you will be shown mercy; with what
> measure you measure out it will be measured again to you; and

---

Plain, 614–616.

106. BDAG, χαρίζομαι.

blessed are the poor and those being persecuted for the sake of righteousness; for theirs is the kingdom of God. (Polycarp, *Philippians*, 2.3)

Both of these passages are, in all likelihood, independent of Matthew and Luke and/or their common source (Q for example) and seem to be drawing from their own independent source (literary or otherwise).[107] We can ascertain their independence simply by noticing the inclusion of mercy (which is found in Luke 6:36; but not in the "do this, and it will be done to you" pattern found in verses 37–38 of the Sermon, nor in Clement's and Polycarp's versions) and kindness in the formulas. These passages therefore give us early independent attestation, not only of the teachings found in Luke 6:37–38, but also of their attribution to Jesus; and—at least in the case of Polycarp—we have these teachings linked up with a version of the blessings.

The word used for "release" (ἀπολύετε) in verse 37 of the Sermon may well bring us back to Jesus's mission statement in Luke 4:18–19, where he mixes a line from Isaiah 58:6 with his quotation of Isaiah 61:1–2 (to let the oppressed go free). Right before the part of Isaiah 58:6 that Jesus quotes it says:

rather loose every bond of injustice; undo the knots of contracts made by force;

ἀλλὰ λῦε πάντα σύνδεσμον ἀδικίας, διάλυε στραγγαλιὰς βιαίων συναλλαγμάτων.

Some scholars have seen a connection between the use of ἀπολύετε in the Sermon on the Plain with λῦε and διάλυε in Isaiah 58.[108] The entire verse in Isaiah 58:6 reads:

I have not chosen such a fast, says the Lord; rather loose every bond of injustice; undo the knots of contracts made by force; let the oppressed go free, and tear up every unjust note.

And Isaiah 61:1–2 says:

The spirit of the Lord is upon me, because he has anointed me; he has sent me to bring good news to the poor, to heal the

---

107. Allison, *Constructing Jesus*, 323–328; Bellinzoni, "The Gospel of Luke in the Apostolic Fathers," in Gregory and Tuckett, *Trajectories through the New Testament and the Apostolic Fathers*, 53–54; 60.

108. Tuckett, *Q and the History of Early Christianity*, 430–431.

brokenhearted, to proclaim release to the captives and recovery of sight to the blind, to summon the acceptable year of the Lord and the day of retribution, to comfort all who mourn.

If we accept this as the context, then we can make sense of the commandment in verse 37 of the Sermon within the context of the whole Sermon, along with the general theme of Jesus's ministry starting with his declaration in Luke 4:18–19. To "forgive" (ἀπολύετε) is to release—as one would do during both the Sabbatical year and the Jubilee year—debts that result in oppression and bondage, as well as those in bondage.[109] If this connection holds, we can interpret "release" in verse 37 with the "Justice for the poor" commandment being appealed to in Isaiah 58, this would fit with what comes next: give (δίδοτε). If the Sabbatical year legislation is followed and one releases his debtors, his debts would also be released. Just as the first two exhortations in verse 37 likely have duel applications—both communal and eschatological—it is also likely that the second two exhortations likewise have duel applications. When the Jubilee and Sabbatical year laws are practiced, and you release your fellow's debts and those in bondage, it will be released to you both by your fellow Israelites and by God. If you give to others, then God will give to you, and your fellow Israelites will give to you as well when you are in need.

As we talked about earlier, there can be certain hierarchical connotations to gift giving in that the receiver would be thought of as inferior unless he reciprocates in kind (or more). However, using the Sabbatical year legislation as the background, we see how this would not be the case in the Sermon's admonition to give. As we saw earlier, Deuteronomy 15 puts giving (δίδωμι) and lending (δανίζω) together—distinguishing, yet relating the two— however, their being placed together implies that both of them are included in the release, both formal debts, and informal obligations of reciprocation that come with gift giving are to be released. This is one reason that Jesus can expect his disciples to follow the admonition in verse 30 and give to everyone (παντὶ): the power relations and implications of inequality that might arise from gift giving will be undone in the release.

The second part of the verse explains what kind of return one can expect: "A good measure, pressed down, shaken, overflowing, in YOUR bosom—for the measure YOU measure out, it will be measured in return to YOU The four-fold exhortation is matched with a reward described as

109. Evans, *Saint Luke,* 337.

excessive in four different ways.[110] The image here is not merely that of excess abundance; it is that of immeasurability.[111] This saying is paralleled in both Mark 4:24, and Matthew 7:2. In Matthew 7:2 the saying is used in the context of judging others and hypocrisy. In Mark 4:24 it is used in a context which seems to be about receiving knowledge. However, in Mark the phrase "and still more will be given you" (καὶ προστεθήσεται ὑμῖν) is included, implying the same notion of excess. Luke however, uses the phrase in the context of giving, which itself is used in the commandments of Deuteronomy 15.

This brings us back to the interpretation of the usury laws by Jesus as recorded in the Sermon on the Plain; as opposed to the interpretation of the Rabbis, specifically Hillel, in the Mishnah. If we recall, Hillel (along with the other pharisaic rabbis) interpreted the usury laws primarily using Leviticus 25 as a framework, and he primarily interpreted them as laws intended to prevent profit from being taken from loans, loans ought to be equal exchanges (Mishnah, *Baba Metzia.* 5.1;9). Jesus, on the other hand, used Deuteronomy 15 as his main framework—leading to the notion that loans ought to be given without the thought of return, without measurement, as though the release was coming—they should be given as a way to build up and support the community: building a "communist" ethic within the community.

As we read earlier, the main difference between a "debt" and an "obligation" is that the former can be quantified and the latter cannot.[112] In verse 38 of the Sermon we get the promise: if you follow the Sabbatical year ethic, and lend without measuring, without expecting a return, and give to all who are in need, others will do the same. The immeasurable excess that "they" will give to you is precisely what you are giving to them. It is not the amount that is being matched, it is the relationship, that of trust and non-contractual mutual aid. In other words, if you treat people as though you are in a communist relationship with them, as opposed to a hierarchical or exchange relationship; they will treat you the same way. The unmeasured sharing—which is seen as excessive to someone who thinks in terms of exchange—is an unmeasured sharing which you participate in along with others; it is the building of a relationship, a community, in which sharing

110. Evans, *Saint Luke,* 337.

111. Betz, *A commentary on the Sermon on the Mount, including the Sermon on the Plain,* 617–618.

112. Graeber, *Debt,* 21.

is done without concern for exchange. In a sense, this is a more excessive version of the "from each according to his ability, to each according to his need" maxim of communism.

The connection with non-retaliation (verses 27–29) is clear when one understands the connection between violence and economic calculation. We have already discussed this connection in that an assumption of non-violence is necessary for communist relationships; and exchange relationships are reserved for situations where violence can be expected. However, the connection between violence and exchange is not just in the shifting of social relationship types from communism to exchange; it is actually innate to the exchange relationship type itself. David Graeber says:

> However, when one looks a little closer, one discovers that these two elements—the violence and the quantification—are intimately linked. In fact it's almost impossible to find one without the other. French usurers had powerful friends and enforcers, capable of bullying even Church authorities. How else would they have collected debts that were technically illegal?[113]

In his work on Bureaucracy he writes:

> We are now so used to the idea that we at least *could* call the police to resolve virtually any difficult circumstance that many of us find it difficult to even imagine what people would have done before this was possible. Because, in fact, for the vast majority of people throughout history—even those who lived in large cities—there were simply no authorities to call in such circumstances. Or, at least, no impersonal bureaucratic ones who were, like the modern police, empowered to impose arbitrary resolutions backed by the threat of force.[114]

And later:

> All of these are institutions involved in the allocation of resources within a system of property rights regulated and guaranteed by governments in a system that ultimately rests on the threat of force. "Force" in turn is just a euphemistic way to refer to violence: that is, the ability to call up people dressed in uniforms, willing to threaten to hit others over the head with wooden sticks.[115]

113. Graeber, *Debt,* 14.
114. Graeber, *Utopia of Rules,* 22.
115. Graeber, *Utopia of Rules,* 37.

So even in societies where random violence by strangers is not an ever-present threat, such as a society with the "Pax Romana," the economic relationships of exchange are still completely dependent on the threat of violence; the only difference is that this violence is outsourced to the state. So here we see that the non-violence in the Sermon's message and the call to lend without expecting a return are absolutely related, and the latter is dependent on the former. In Jesus's promoting non-violence, forgiveness, and non-quantified, non-reciprocal, mutual obligations—I am claiming that the Sermon on the Plain is promoting a certain kind of relationship: a communist relationship; over other kinds of relationships like hierarchy or exchange.

Summation

The ethics portion of the Sermon takes general Torah principles and brings them to their logical conclusion, doing so in a way that may seem extreme on the surface. Ultimately, the purpose of these ethics is to build a community faithful to the eschatological message of the blessings and woes found in verses 20–26. These ethics may at first seem near impossible, especially given the social situation of the time; however, the last couple of verses of the ethics show how Jesus's contention is that not only are they not impossible, they result in a community of generous abundance.

The ideological systems of honor and benefaction, imported from the Greco-Roman world, are banished from Jesus's ethical system, explicitly. This is an ethical system where normal games of honor, mediated by violence and strategic giving, are simply not played. They are instead replaced with an ethic grounded in principles such as those found in Deuteronomy 15. The economic principles of the Sermon are firmly based on Deuteronomy 15, with its debt release and command to lend despite the release. This ties right back in with the eschatological vision in the blessings and woes. If the *eschaton* is modeled after things like the Jubilee (which we see in some of the Qumran documents), then the connection between the eschatological social reversal and the concomitant economic ethics fit together perfectly. Once one understands the implications of the Jubilee/Sabbatical based *eschaton*—a cancelation of all debts, and a reversal of the social system—one can dispense with honor systems, with benefaction systems, and with calculated market systems. This also does away with honor systems in a different sense. Given that one who attempts to humiliate you is likely going to be on the losing end of the *eschaton*, one can simply respond in a way that attempts to build community, rather than fight for a place in a system which is on its way out.

Jesus anticipates that out of this kind of ethic, a community will be established which will model the age to come and be prepared for its coming. The *eschaton* changes everything. Hellenistic philosophy and Pharisaic rulings (much less apocalyptic than Jesus's thinking) attempted to make ethical systems that work within the social context, Jesus however is making an ethic that subverts the context because he knows a new context is coming, and the ethics he commands are for that new context. These ethics are also the way to build a new community that anticipates that new context and lives it out in the present.

That being said, the Sermon on the Plain does not end with the ethics. In verses 39–49 we get a series of parables whose purpose is to anticipate problems that will arise within an eschatological community with a Jubilee and Sabbatical ethic, and to deal with them.

5

The Parables

The Parables

FROM VERSES 39–49 WE have five parables. In verses 39–40 we have two
parables which more or less make the same point: the people need instruction. In verses 41–42 we have the straw-in-the-eye parable about hypocrisy.
In verses 43–45 we have the parable of the fine tree and the rotten tree,
dealing with the relationship between thought and word. Verses 39–42
are rules for the community of disciples;[1] whereas verses 43–45 are rules
for the disciple's relationship to himself, put in the descriptive rather than
the prescriptive form.[2] In verse 46 we have the main point of the parables.
In verses 47–49 we have the parable of the houses and their foundations,
dealing with the relationship between hearing and doing, and the absolute
necessity of action.[3] These parables are focused especially on ethical praxis
rather than ethical theory.

Verses 39–40 say:

> Then he also spoke a parable to them, a blind man is not able to
> guide a blind man, is he? Will not both of them fall into a pit? A

---

1. Betz, *A commentary on the Sermon on the Mount, including the Sermon on the
Plain*, 619.

2. Betz, *A commentary on the Sermon on the Mount, including the Sermon on the
Plain*, 628.

3. Betz, *A commentary on the Sermon on the Mount, including the Sermon on the
Plain*, 636.

disciple is not above the teacher, but everyone being fully qualified will be as his teacher.

Εἶπεν δὲ καὶ παραβολὴν αὐτοῖς· μήτι δύναται τυφλὸς τυφλὸν ὁδηγεῖν; οὐχὶ ἀμφότεροι εἰς βόθυνον ἐμπεσοῦνται; οὐκ ἔστιν μαθητὴς ὑπὲρ τὸν διδάσκαλον· κατηρτισμένος δὲ πᾶς ἔσται ὡς ὁ διδάσκαλος αὐτοῦ.

This parable is set in a poetic structure, with ten words divided into two phrases of five words each. The imagery of the blind teacher was well known in the ancient world and was often used as a defense of education.[4] One use of this imagery in the first part of the first-century in the Jewish world is that of Philo, who uses the imagery in criticizing the greedy:

> But if any persons, utterly disregarding the true wealth of nature, pursue instead the riches of vain opinions, relying on those riches which are blind instead of on those which are gifted with acute sight, and taking a guide for their road who is himself crippled, such men must of necessity fall down. (Philo, *On Virtues*, 2 [Yong])

Philo's use of this parable likely had its origins in one of Philo's biggest influences—Plato—who, like Philo, uses the imagery in reference to greed:

> don't suppose that such a man pays any attention to education. Not in my view, for, if he did, he wouldn't have chosen a blind leader for his chorus and honored him most. (Plato, *Republic*, 8.554b)

If we look at the parallel in Mathew, the application is made to the Pharisees:

> Let them [the Pharisees] alone; they are blind guides of the blind. And if one blind person guides another, both will fall into a pit."

ἄφετε αὐτούς· τυφλοί εἰσιν ὁδηγοὶ [τυφλῶν]· τυφλὸς δὲ τυφλὸν ἐὰν ὁδηγῇ, ἀμφότεροι εἰς βόθυνον πεσοῦνται. (Matt 15:14)

There is however, no trace of any anti-Pharisaic polemic in Luke's version,[5] nor would it make any sense if the blind guide was intended to represent wealth. Verse 40 of the Sermon clarifies the point of the parable: the teacher is above the student and thus the student needs to learn from the teacher in order to become like him; a student cannot learn from a fellow student

---

4. Betz, *A commentary on the Sermon on the Mount, including the Sermon on the Plain,* 620–621.

5. Marshall, *The Gospel of Luke,* 269.

what he can learn from a good teacher. The saying in verse 40 is also paralleled in Matthew,[6] which, in its context, says:

> and you will be hated by all because of my name. But the one who endures to the end will be saved. When they persecute you in one town, flee to the next; for truly I tell you, you will not have gone through all the towns of Israel before the Son of Man comes.
>
> "A disciple is not above the teacher (Οὐκ ἔστιν μαθητὴς ὑπὲρ τὸν διδάσκαλον), nor a slave above the master; it is enough for the disciple to be like the teacher (ἀρκετὸν τῷ μαθητῇ ἵνα γένηται ὡς ὁ διδάσκαλος αὐτοῦ καὶ ὁ δοῦλος), and the slave like the master. If they have called the master of the house Beelzebul, how much more will they malign those of his household! (Matt 10:22–25)

This use of the saying in Mathew makes a completely different point than the use of it in the Sermon on the Plain: rather than being about expecting persecution (which is what the saying is about in Matthew); the Sermon on the Plain's usage of the saying is to point out the need a student has for a teacher. Not just for the sake of an education, but to be "as his teacher" (ἔσται ὡς ὁ διδάσκαλος αὐτοῦ); in this case, like Jesus.[7] Although this could be seen as simply a plea for education—which would point to this parable being aimed at a Hellenistic audience, since Jews already had a high view of education[8]—the fact that, for the Sermon, the purpose of the education is to become like Jesus may hint at a different interpretation (of which there are many).[9] One possible interpretation could be that Jesus was taking a general plea for education, but then making the point that one should be careful who one chooses as a teacher (without specifically pointing out the Pharisees). This would actually bring the meaning in line with Matthew's usage of the parable. The Sermon on the Plain makes the point that one needs a teacher and that one should be careful about who one chooses as a teacher; and Matthew uses this general principle in two specific instances: do not choose the Pharisees who are blind guides, and by choosing Jesus one is choosing to go through persecution. Here we see that although Luke is making a different point in using this parable than Matthew makes in

6. The verse is also found in the Gospel of Thomas 26; 34.

7. Evans, *Saint Luke*, 338.

8. Betz, *A commentary on the Sermon on the Mount, including the Sermon on the Plain*, 621.

9. Betz, *A commentary on the Sermon on the Mount, including the Sermon on the Plain*, 623–624.

both his usages, Luke's point is compatible with Matthew's two points; and both of Matthew's points are faithful to the original concept. The Sermon on the Plain includes the idea that the student has to be "fully qualified" (καταρτίζω), which has the implication of having gone through, and completed, the training.[10] The idea here is that in order to be "like Jesus," one has to complete the training, which involves following the commandments set out in the ethical portion of the Sermon: one is expected to learn the teachings and practice them.

In verses 41–42 we have the famous "speck in your brother's eye" parable:

> Why do you see the speck in your brother's eye, but the beam in your own eye you do not consider? How are you able to say to your brother "brother, allow me to get out the speck in your eye," while you yourself are not seeing the beam in your eye. Hypocrite, first get the beam out from your eye, and then you will see clearly to get out the speck in your brother's eye.

> Τί δὲ βλέπεις τὸ κάρφος τὸ ἐν τῷ ὀφθαλμῷ τοῦ ἀδελφοῦ σου, τὴν δὲ δοκὸν τὴν ἐν τῷ ἰδίῳ ὀφθαλμῷ οὐ κατανοεῖς; πῶς δύνασαι λέγειν τῷ ἀδελφῷ σου· ἀδελφέ, ἄφες ἐκβάλω τὸ κάρφος τὸ ἐν τῷ ὀφθαλμῷ σου, αὐτὸς τὴν ἐν τῷ ὀφθαλμῷ σου δοκὸν οὐ βλέπων; ὑποκριτά, ἔκβαλε πρῶτον τὴν δοκὸν ἐκ τοῦ ὀφθαλμοῦ σου, καὶ τότε διαβλέψεις τὸ κάρφος τὸ ἐν τῷ ὀφθαλμῷ τοῦ ἀδελφοῦ σου ἐκβαλεῖν.

This is paralleled in Matthew's Sermon on the Mount (7:3–5) with almost the exact same wording and with no different context. The meaning in both Matthew and Luke is very clear: you are in no position to judge your neighbor. In both versions there is a shift in the Greek from "seeing" (βλέπω) the speck in your neighbor's eye to "considering" or "perceiving" (κατανοέω) the log in your own eye, the shift indicates a move from observing others to introspection.[11] This saying also appears in the Baba Bathra tractate of the Babylonian Talmud; however, the Talmud uses the saying to make the opposite point from the one Jesus is recorded as making. The context for the saying in the Talmud is the times when Job lived:

> Rabbi Elazar says: Job lived in the days of the judging of the Judges, as it is stated in connection with Job: "Behold, all you yourselves

10. Betz, *A commentary on the Sermon on the Mount, including the Sermon on the Plain*, 624–625.

11. Betz, *A commentary on the Sermon on the Mount, including the Sermon on the Plain*, 626.

have seen it; why then have you become altogether vain?" Which generation was completely vain? You must say it was the generation of the judging of the Judges, when the people judged the Judges, as will be explained shortly.

. . .

Rabbi Yoḥanan says: What is the meaning of that which is written: "And it happened in the days of the judging of the Judges"? This indicates a generation that judged its judges. If a judge would say to the defendant standing before him: Remove the splinter from between your eyes, meaning rid yourself of some minor infraction, the defendant would say to him: Remove the beam from between your eyes, meaning you have committed far more severe sins. If the judge would say to him: "Your silver is become dross," meaning your coins are counterfeit, the defendant would say to him: "Your wine is mixed with water," meaning you yourself dilute your wine with water and sell it. Since nobody behaved in proper manner, the judges were unable to judge. (Babylonian Talmud, *Baba Bathra.* 15b)

And similarly, in tractate Arachin it says:

Rabbi Tarfon said, I wonder whether there is any one in this generation who accepts reproof, for if one says to him: Remove the mote from between your eyes, he would answer: Remove the beam from between your eyes! (Babylonian Talmud, *Arachin.* 16b)

The point Rabbi Yohanan and Rabbi Tarfon are making is completely the opposite of Jesus's point. The rabbis take the person who says "remove the splinter (or mote) from between your eyes" as behaving improperly because he is subverting the correct order of things. In a sense, the rabbis are saying that we need judges who are able to judge, if the person being judged is always judging the judge there can be no order. The vision of Rabbi Yohanan is that of official judges during the time of Job; that of Rabbi Tarfon seems to be that of wise people reproving others who are going astray. Either way, the message is not that hypocrisy is good; it is rather that constantly looking for hypocrisy in order to avoid judgment is wrong. For the rabbis, judgment or reproof are good and necessary; and if there are people who reject judgment due to some real or perceived hypocrisy, they are acting improperly and ruining the generation that they live in.

We cannot be sure if the saying came first from Jesus or the rabbis. However, if the saying originated with the rabbis; then what Jesus is doing is quite subversive: he is reversing the moral message of the saying.

Rather than say that judgment is necessary and thus one should not charge hypocrisy to avoid judgment; he accepts that hypocrisy would invalidate a judgment and then chooses to simply get rid of judgment altogether. The question of what is primary, the office or the person holding the office, is a question that constantly comes up in history; within Christian history it notably became a big issue during the Donatist controversy. The rabbis take the position that the office outweighs the officeholder, and the rulings outweigh the personal integrity of the one giving the ruling. Jesus takes the reverse position: the office is dependent on the integrity of the officeholder. But rather than insisting that the office holder have perfect integrity, Jesus argues that we should get rid of the office completely.

The term "hypocrite," (ὑποκριτά) in the gospels is usually reserved for outsiders (Pharisees for example),[12] but in this case it is anyone who assumes the right to sit in judgement over anyone else. The term came to be used in the Hellenistic world to refer to an orator or an actor on a stage; the implication in the gospels is that the "hypocrite" is play-acting—and in the case of the Sermon on the Plain—play-acting as a judge."[13] As we saw previously, the audience of the Sermon is mixed, with both the lower classes, the poor, along with those of some power and means; the audience for this statement would have to be those who had positions where they would sit in judgment over others, perhaps actual judges in the Sanhedrin, or other religious authorities such as the Pharisees. They are, according to Jesus, play-acting piety in their judgment; while they are actually impious, and would have to fix their own impiety before they have the right to judge others.[14] The problem is that, in order to fix their impiety, they would have to refrain from judging others. Therefore, the only way to have the right to judge others would be not to do so. This would effectively take away the religious power of the Pharisees and the judicial power of the Sanhedrin.

This parable is essentially an explanation of verse 37, where it says again:

> Also do not judge, and YOU will not be judged; and do not condemn, and YOU will not be condemned; release, and YOU will be released,

12. Betz, *A commentary on the Sermon on the Mount, including the Sermon on the Plain*, 627.

13. Fitzmyer, *The Gospel According to Luke I–IX*, 642.

14. Marshall, *The Gospel of Luke*, 271.

Καὶ μὴ κρίνετε, καὶ οὐ μὴ κριθῆτε· καὶ μὴ καταδικάζετε, καὶ οὐ μὴ καταδικασθῆτε. ἀπολύετε, καὶ ἀπολυθήσεσθε·

The word κρίνω (judge) can be used both in the personal sense, and the judicial sense; so it can refer to an individual expressing an opinion about someone else or finding fault with someone else, and it can also refer to a judicial process.[15] The word κατεδίκασα (condemn) is usually used as a judicial condemnation.[16] Given this (along with the fact that the rabbis used the saying in both the judicial sense and the personal sense) it would seem that Jesus is not only rejecting personal judgment of others, but even calling to question the validity of the courts themselves due to their hypocrisy. This statement that Jesus is recorded as making may seem rather extreme, but given the context of the Sermon—with its demands to lend without expecting a return and its repudiation of the concept of honor—it fits right in.

The next parable we find is that of the trees and their fruit in verses 43–45:

> For no fine tree is producing rotten fruit; on the other hand, nor does a rotten tree produce fine fruit. For each tree is known from its own fruit—because they do not gather figs from thorns, neither do they cut grapes from thorn-bushes. A good person brings forth good from the good treasure from his heart, and the wicked brings forth wickedness from his wicked [[heart]]—for out of the abundance of his heart his mouth speaks.

> Οὐ γάρ ἐστιν δένδρον καλὸν ποιοῦν καρπὸν σαπρόν, οὐδὲ πάλιν δένδρον σαπρὸν ποιοῦν καρπὸν καλόν. ἕκαστον γὰρ δένδρον ἐκ τοῦ ἰδίου καρποῦ γινώσκεται· οὐ γὰρ ἐξ ἀκανθῶν συλλέγουσιν σῦκα οὐδὲ ἐκ βάτου σταφυλὴν τρυγῶσιν. ὁ ἀγαθὸς ἄνθρωπος ἐκ τοῦ ἀγαθοῦ θησαυροῦ τῆς καρδίας προφέρει τὸ ἀγαθόν, καὶ ὁ πονηρὸς ἐκ τοῦ πονηροῦ προφέρει τὸ πονηρόν· ἐκ γὰρ περισσεύματος καρδίας λαλεῖ τὸ στόμα αὐτοῦ.

Matthew uses this parable on two different occasions, one in the Sermon on the Mount:

> "Beware of false prophets, who come to you in sheep's clothing but inwardly are ravenous wolves. You will know them by their fruits (ἀπὸ τῶν καρπῶν αὐτῶν ἐπιγνώσεσθε αὐτούς). Are grapes gathered from thorns, or figs from thistles? In the same way, every good tree bears good fruit, but the bad tree bears bad fruit (Οὕτως πᾶν

---

15. BDAG, κρίνω.
16. BDAG, κατεδίκασα.

δένδρον ἀγαθὸν καρποὺς καλοὺς ποιεῖ, τὸ δὲ σαπρὸν δένδρον καρποὺς πονηροὺς ποιεῖ). A good tree cannot bear bad fruit, nor can a bad tree bear good fruit (οὐ δύναται δένδρον ἀγαθὸν καρποὺς πονηροὺς ποιεῖν οὐδὲ δένδρον σαπρὸν καρποὺς καλοὺς ποιεῖν). Every tree that does not bear good fruit is cut down and thrown into the fire (πᾶν δένδρον μὴ ποιοῦν καρπὸν καλὸν ἐκκόπτεται καὶ εἰς πῦρ βάλλεται). Thus you will know them by their fruits (ἄρα γε ἀπὸ τῶν καρπῶν αὐτῶν ἐπιγνώσεσθε αὐτούς). (Matt 7:15–20)

And another in a dialogue with the Pharisees:

"Either make the tree good, and its fruit good; or make the tree bad, and its fruit bad; for the tree is known by its fruit (Η ποιήσατε τὸ δένδρον καλὸν καὶ τὸν καρπὸν αὐτοῦ καλόν, ἢ ποιήσατε τὸ δένδρον σαπρὸν καὶ τὸν καρπὸν αὐτοῦ σαπρόν· ἐκ γὰρ τοῦ καρποῦ τὸ δένδρον γινώσκεται). You brood of vipers! How can you speak good things, when you are evil? For out of the abundance of the heart the mouth speaks. The good person brings good things out of a good treasure, and the evil person brings evil things out of an evil treasure. I tell you, on the day of judgment you will have to give an account for every careless word you utter; for by your words you will be justified, and by your words you will be condemned." (Matt 12:33–37)

The verse is also paralleled in the Gospel of Thomas:

His disciples said to him, "Who are you to say these things to us?"
"You don't understand who I am from what I say to you.
Rather, you have become like the Judeans, for they love the tree but hate its fruit, or they love the fruit but hate the tree." Jesus said, "Whoever blasphemes against the Father will be forgiven, and whoever blasphemes against the son will be forgiven, but whoever blasphemes against the Holy Spirit will not be forgiven, either on earth or in heaven." Jesus said, "Grapes are not harvested from thorn trees, nor are figs gathered from thistles, for they yield no fruit. Good persons produce good from what they've stored up; bad persons produce evil from the wickedness they've stored up in their hearts, and say evil things. For from the overflow of the heart they produce evil." (Gospel of Thomas 43–45)

Both of Matthew's uses of this parable are aimed at specific groups: false prophets in chapter 7, and the Pharisees in chapter 12. Thomas's use of this parable is against the Judeans in saying 43; but dealing more in general (good persons as opposed to bad persons) in saying 45.

In the Sermon on the Plain however, the application is general: it is the good person (ὁ ἀγαθὸς ἄνθρωπος) as opposed to the wicked one (ὁ πονηρὸς). Ultimately, this is about speech, and how speech reflects on a person's heart.[17] This is the same basic application as Matthew 12 and the Gospel of Thomas. However, in the Sermon on the Mount in Matthew 7 the application is not completely clear: the fruit could be speech or works. But given the lack of reference to speaking or the tongue, it is fair to say that it is more likely referring to works. The image of fruit as a figure for works is common in the Hebrew bible and would have been recognizable to an audience familiar with the biblical tradition.[18] The audience of the saying in the Sermon on the Plain is likely those who are following, or are considering to follow, Jesus; as opposed to an outside group. This parable would, in a sense, follow from Jesus's rejection of judgment in the previous parable; at least in the individual sense of judging others (rather than the judicial system sense). The disciples are to check their own heart before they speak in order to make sure they have the correct motivations, to make sure the produce of their fruits—their words or their teachings—will be good ones.[19] Interestingly, it seems as though verses 41–42 could be connected to verses 43–45 by the similarities of the catchwords "speck" (κάρφος in verses 41–42) and "fruit" (καρπός in verses 43–45). The connection being (other than the wordplay that seems to be going on between κάρφος and καρπός) that introspection into one's own character is vital to, and logically prior to, how one acts in the world.[20] A rather similar parable is found in the rabbinic tradition. The Mishnah records a saying of Rabbi Eleazar which says:

> He whose wisdom is more abundant than his works, to what is he like? To a tree whose branches are abundant but whose roots are few; and the wind comes and uproots it and overturns it, as it is written, He shall be like a tamarisk in the desert and shall not see when good cometh; but shall inhabit the parched places in the wilderness. But he whose works are more abundant than his wisdom, to what is he like? To a tree whose branches are few but whose roots are many; so that even if all the winds in the world come and blow against it, it cannot be stirred from its place, as it is written,

17. Marshall, *The Gospel of Luke*, 273.

18. Fitzmyer, *The Gospel According to Luke I–IX*, 643. For example: Hosea 10:13; Isaiah 3:10; Jeremiah 17:10; 21:14.

19. Marshall, *The Gospel of Luke*, 271.

20. Betz, *A commentary on the Sermon on the Mount, including the Sermon on the Plain*, 628–630.

> He shall be as a tree planted by the waters, and that spreadeth out his roots by the river, and shall not fear when heat cometh, and his leaf shall be green; and shall not be careful in the year of drought, neither shall cease from yielding fruit. (Mishnah, *Aboth*. 3.18)

Here we see a similar agricultural metaphor being used, this time comparing the root and the branches of the tree; but the parable also quotes a verse from Jeremiah 17 that equates spiritual blessings with the yielding of fruit. The point being made with Rabbi Eleazar's parable is similar to the point being made in the parable we will look at next in verses: 46–49. We see that in the time of Jesus it was common to use "tree" parables in comparing things like: wisdom and works (Rabbi Eleazar), prophecy and outcome (Matthew 7), and one's heart condition and words (Luke 6, Matthew 12, Gospel of Thomas 43–45).

The last parable is about obedience to Jesus's words: the parable of the two houses with different foundations in verses 46–49:

> But why do YOU call me "lord lord," and YOU do not do what I say; Everyone coming to me and hearing my words and doing them—I will show YOU whom he is like—he is like a man building up a house who dug and went deep and laid a foundation upon the rock. But with the coming of the flood, the river bursts against that house; and was not able to shake it due to its having been built well. But the one having heard and not doing is like a man that having built up a house upon the ground without a foundation, which the river burst against, and it immediately collapsed, and the ruin of that house came to be great.

> Τί δέ με καλεῖτε· κύριε κύριε, καὶ οὐ ποιεῖτε ἃ λέγω; Πᾶς ὁ ἐρχόμενος πρός με καὶ ἀκούων μου τῶν λόγων καὶ ποιῶν αὐτούς, ὑποδείξω ὑμῖν τίνι ἐστὶν ὅμοιος· ὅμοιός ἐστιν ἀνθρώπῳ οἰκοδομοῦντι οἰκίαν ὃς ἔσκαψεν καὶ ἐβάθυνεν καὶ ἔθηκεν θεμέλιον ἐπὶ τὴν πέτραν· πλημμύρης δὲ γενομένης προσέρηξεν ὁ ποταμὸς τῇ οἰκίᾳ ἐκείνῃ, καὶ οὐκ ἴσχυσεν σαλεῦσαι αὐτὴν διὰ τὸ καλῶς οἰκοδομῆσθαι αὐτήν. ὁ δὲ ἀκούσας καὶ μὴ ποιήσας ὅμοιός ἐστιν ἀνθρώπῳ οἰκοδομήσαντι οἰκίαν ἐπὶ τὴν γῆν χωρὶς θεμελίου, ᾗ προσέρηξεν ὁ ποταμός, καὶ εὐθὺς συνέπεσεν καὶ ἐγένετο τὸ ῥῆγμα τῆς οἰκίας ἐκείνης μέγα.

This parable is paralleled in the Sermon on the Mount:

> "Not everyone who says to me, 'Lord, Lord, (κύριε κύριε)' will enter the kingdom of heaven, but only the one who does the will of my Father in heaven (ἀλλ᾽ ὁ ποιῶν τὸ θέλημα τοῦ πατρός μου τοῦ ἐν τοῖς οὐρανοῖς). On that day many will say to me, 'Lord, Lord, did

we not prophesy in your name, and cast out demons in your name, and do many deeds of power in your name?' Then I will declare to them, 'I never knew you; go away from me, you evildoers.'

"Everyone then who hears these words of mine and acts on them (Πᾶς οὖν ὅστις ἀκούει μου τοὺς λόγους τούτους καὶ ποιεῖ αὐτούς) will be like a wise man who built his house on rock. The rain fell, the floods came, and the winds blew and beat on that house, but it did not fall, because it had been founded on rock. And everyone who hears these words of mine and does not act on them (Καὶ πᾶς ὁ ἀκούων μου τοὺς λόγους τούτους καὶ μὴ ποιῶν αὐτούς) will be like a foolish man who built his house on sand. The rain fell, and the floods came, and the winds blew and beat against that house, and it fell—and great was its fall!" (Matt 7:21–27)

This ending should put to rest any reading of the Sermon on the Plain that attempts to minimize the commandments by saying they are hyperbolic or simply about one's heart condition. The point is clear: this sermon is to be heard and put into practice.[21] One aspect of this parable that stands out is Jesus being called "lord lord" (κύριε κύριε). The double form here is rather common in Jewish literature; and is used quite often in Luke's writings. The use of "lord" here is in no way promoting some kind of high Christology, and it corresponds to the Aramaic term *mari*, as opposed to being a divine name replacement or some other divine title. The title of κύριος however, does indicate that Jesus was thought of as higher than a rabbi, or a teacher (διδάσκαλος). This is also seen by the fact that Jesus demands obedience: the audience is to hear his words and do them (ἀκούων μου τῶν λόγων καὶ ποιῶν αὐτούς). This is opposed to Matthew's much more modest "doing the will of my father" (ποιῶν τὸ θέλημα τοῦ πατρός μου).[22] There is no reason to assume that the more modest version in Matthew is more primitive because of its being directed towards the Father's will (rather than Jesus's commandments) given that the term *mari* need not demand a high Christology and that we already have read Jesus taking it upon himself to give commandments that seem to go beyond normal Torah regulations earlier in the Sermon. The Sermon on the Plain, as opposed to Matthew's version, puts more focus on the actual activity of building the house in describing the man "who dug and went deep and laid a foundation upon the rock"

---

21. Marshall, *The Gospel of Luke*, 273–274.
22. Marshall, *The Gospel of Luke*, 274–275; Evans, *Saint Luke*, 340.

(ὃς ἔσκαψεν καὶ ἐβάθυνεν καὶ ἔθηκεν θεμέλιον ἐπὶ τὴν πέτραν).[23] In focusing on the actual building activity itself, Jesus puts an emphasis on the activity of obedience; rather than just the choice of where to put one's foundation.

It seems here that the difference between the two builders is a difference between obedience and disobedience: the one founding his house on a rock is the one who is obedient to Jesus's commandments; whereas the one building his house without foundation is the one who is not. The outcome is survival for the former, and disaster for the latter. The disaster being predicted is likely eschatological,[24] which would link the end of the Sermon up with the blessings and woes in the beginning, as well as provide an eschatological motivation for the entire ethical framework.

Summation

Although each parable has a different specific purpose, they all have a similar message: these ethics are normative, they are not suggestions, nor are they theoretical ideals; they are commandments that must be not only obeyed but must be actually built into one's own character. The parables highlight the need for being taught, and the need for this teaching to change a person. They also highlight the implications of Jesus's ethics on interpersonal relationships. Ultimately, they are about the fact that what Jesus's ethics demand is rightly motivated obedience. This brings us back to the eschatological reversal and the fourth blessing and woe. The reason the ones who are on the side of the Son of Man are hated, excluded, reproached, and have their name denounced as wicked, is that their being on the side of the Son of Man has real world implications that have concrete social effects.

23. Betz, *A commentary on the Sermon on the Mount, including the Sermon on the Plain*, 639.

24. Fitzmyer, *The Gospel According to Luke I–IX*, 644; Evans, *Saint Luke*, 339.

6

The Aftermath

Early Christian Application

THERE WERE TWO WAYS the early Christians (I will be focusing on the first two centuries of Christian history here) applied the teachings of the Sermon on the Plain that I want to focus on in this section: communism and pacifism. I have written on the subject of communism in my book *All Things in Common: The Economic Practices of the Early Christians* (2017, Resource Publications) where I lay out the evidence for early Christian communism in detail, along with a reconstruction of that communism. I will not restate the argument and reconstruction of early Christian communism here; rather, I will summarize the practices and demonstrate their connection to the Sermon on the Plain.

As I pointed out earlier, but which bears repeating, the term "communism" in this context is being used in its economic-anthropological sense; not its modern political sense. In the economic-anthropological sense "communism" is not an economic system or a political ideology; but rather a kind of social relationship.[1] Communism in this sense basically means any kind of relationship which functions on the moral principle of "from each according to his ability, to each according to his need;" as opposed to "exchange"—which functions on a quid pro quo principle; or "hierarchy"—which functions on a top-down principle.[2] This communist principle can be found almost anywhere: people helping each other with day to day tasks

1. Alan, *Structures of Social Life*, 170.
2. Graeber, *Debt*, 94.

on the street, friends buying each other drinks, neighborhood cook-outs, and so on.[3] In the book *All Things in Common* I label these examples of spontaneous communist relationships "informal communism;" and I distinguish them from "formal communism" which would be communism that includes some kind of regulatory enforcement: such as in a monastery, a public institution, a social insurance system, or a cooperative business.[4]

The early Christians practiced both formal and informal communism all over the Roman Empire, well into the second century, and to a significant degree,[5] so much so that they were actually known for their communism by their enemies. One example of this is the second-century Roman poet Lucian who went so far as to actually claim that the main doctrine of the Christians was holding all things in common, he describes the Christian doctrine saying:

> Furthermore, their first lawgiver persuaded them that they are all brothers of one another after they have transgressed once for all by denying the Greek gods and by worshiping that crucified sophist himself and living under his laws. Therefore they despise all things indiscriminately and consider them common property, receiving such doctrines traditionally without any definite evidence. (Lucian, *The Passing of Peregrinus*, 13 [Harmon])

This communism was practiced to such a degree that, even though private property was not formally abolished, it was as if it had been,[6] which is why Luke makes the claim in Acts 4:32 that "no one claimed ownership over any of their possessions," and why the *Didache* orders "do not claim that anything is your own" (Didache 4.8). The informal communism aspect was the general principle of sharing, which was done to the point to where the verses in Acts 2:42–47; 4:32–37 that claim they held all things in common can be taken almost literally.[7] The "formal communism" aspect was a regular collection of goods which were then used to distribute aid to widows, orphans, prisoners, and the poor in general.[8] This "formal communism" should not be confused with sporadic philanthropy; rather, it

---

3. Graeber, *Debt*, 95.

4. Montero, *All Things in Common*, 25–26.

5. Montero, *All Things in Common*, 69.

6. Montero, *All Things in Common*, 52–53.

7. Montero, *All Things in Common*, 63–64.

8. Montero, *All Things in Common*, 58–60; 73; 80–81.

was something which facilitated a daily distribution of food to widows[9]and which was so generous that it was susceptible to being abused.[10]

How did this happen? A direct connection can be made between the teachings of the Sermon on the Plain, and the later communist practices of the early Christians.[11] In a society that was becoming increasingly commercialized, as was first-century Judea and Galilee, a Jubilee/Sabbatical lending ethic would push the economic culture in the other direction. If the Christians were expecting God's Kingdom to bring about a Jubilee-like *eschaton*, and if they expected that their place in the Kingdom partially depended on their following certain ethical norms based on the Sabbatical year regulations, it is no wonder that they would organize themselves in a way that was contrary to the dominant economic and cultural trends. Lending freely, without calculation, creating mutual obligations, is the basis of a "communist relationship." This is because lending freely, without calculation, and without repayment being secured by threat of force, requires, and fosters, trust.[12]

It is these practices of Christians binding themselves to each other with mutual obligations—lending without expecting a return—that created the communist relationships and communities we find in Acts 2:42–47, Acts 4:32–37, and in Lucian's descriptions of the Christians' doctrines (along with many other places). It is the eschatological vision of Jesus that motivated these practices.

Another outcome of the ethical vision of the Sermon on the Plain is the early Christians' relationship to violence. We know that most of the early Christians in the first two centuries after Jesus were pacifists, or that they at least refrained from doing violence and joining the military.[13] Even Paul remained a pacifist, despite how Romans 13:1–7 is often read. Romans 13:1–7 assumes that the governing authorities are separate from the audience that Paul is writing to, and it assumes that his audience is subject to those governing authorities;[14] whereas the previous verses in 12:9–21 indicate how Paul believes a Christian is to conduct himself; which is to actively love one's enemy, to never avenge oneself, and to live peaceably with

9. Montero, *All Things in Common*, 56–57.

10. Montero, *All Things in Common*, 73–74.

11. Montero, *All Things in Common*, 93.

12. Montero, *All Things in Common*, 91; Graeber, *Debt*, 79.

13. Swift, *The Early Fathers on War and Military Service*, 68–69.

14. Yoder, *The Politics of Jesus*, 203.

all.[15] So Paul is saying that the government authorities act one way—which is their business, and which Christians have nothing to do with other than that they are subject to those authorities—but followers of Christ must act in a different way.

Towards the end of the second century and through the third century there is evidence of some Christians in the military, but that evidence is meager.[16] Nevertheless, in the pre-Constantine Christian literature the early Christian writers were almost unanimously against Christians serving in the military.[17] Justin Martyr, for example, says:

> For from Jerusalem there went out into the world, men, twelve in number, and these illiterate, of no ability in speaking: but by the power of God they proclaimed to every race of men that they were sent by Christ to teach to all the word of God; and we who formerly used to murder one another do not only now refrain from making war upon our enemies, but also, that we may not lie nor deceive our examiners, willingly die confessing Christ. (Justin Martyr, *First Apology*, 39 [Dods and Reith])

Tertullian, echoing the same sentiment says:

> But now inquiry is made about this point, whether a believer may turn himself unto military service, and whether the military may be admitted unto the faith, even the rank and file, or each inferior grade, to whom there is no necessity for taking part in sacrifices or capital punishments. There is no agreement between the divine and the human sacrament, the standard of Christ and the standard of the devil, the camp of light and the camp of darkness. One soul cannot be due to two masters—God and Caesar.
>
> . . .
>
> But how will a Christian man war, nay, how will he serve even in peace, without a sword, which the Lord has taken away? For albeit soldiers had come unto John, and had received the formula of their rule; albeit, likewise, a centurion had believed; still the Lord afterward, in disarming Peter, disarmed every soldier. No dress is lawful among us, if assigned to any unlawful action. (Tertullian, *On Idolatry*, 19 [Thelwall])

In another writing Tertullian says:

---

15. Yoder, *The Politics of Jesus*, 196–197.

16. Swift, *The Early Fathers on War and Military Service*, 69–71.

17. Swift, *The Early Fathers on War and Military Service*, 17–18.

Shall it be held lawful to make an occupation of the sword, when the Lord proclaims that he who uses the sword shall perish by the sword? And shall the son of peace take part in the battle when it does not become him even to sue at law? And shall he apply the chain, and the prison, and the torture, and the punishment, who is not the avenger even of his own wrongs?

. . .

Of course, if faith comes later, and finds any preoccupied with military service, their case is different, as in the instance of those whom John used to receive for baptism, and of those most faithful centurions, I mean the centurion whom Christ approves, and the centurion whom Peter instructs; yet, at the same time, when a man has become a believer, and faith has been sealed, there must be either an immediate abandonment of it, which has been the course with many; or all sorts of quibbling will have to be resorted to in order to avoid offending God, and that is not allowed even outside of military service; or, last of all, for God the fate must be endured which a citizen-faith has been no less ready to accept.

. . .

Indeed, if, putting my strength to the question, I banish from us the military life. (Tertullian, *De Corona*, 11 [Thelwall])

Here we see the clear rule in place, both by Tertullian and Justin Martyr: Christians do not serve in the military, they do not go to war, and they do not kill. Tertullian goes further in explaining that if someone is already serving in the military when he decides to become a Christian, he has two choices: either he abandon military service (taking whatever consequences may come); or he must refrain from doing anything in his service that would violate Christian ethics, that would include doing violence or participating in sacrifices. Basically, the soldier that becomes a Christian would be a soldier in name only or not at all.

Origen agrees with Tertullian and Justin Martyr, saying that Christians do not go to war (Origen, *Against Celsus*, 8.70). Origen also—responding to the anti-Christian philosopher Celsus—addresses Celsus's point that Christians do not fight for the king and are therefore not helping with the maintenance of justice by saying that they do help society and the king by praying (Origen, *Against Celsus*, 8.73). The interesting thing here is that Origen, in defending the Christians against Celsus's charge, does not deny it: it is true that the Christians do not take up arms for the king, but it is also true that they pray for him. This same sentiment is also expressed earlier by Tertullian in his Apology (Tertullian, *Apology*, 30). So, the Christians were not refusing military service because they were anti-Rome, or because they were anti-Caesar—although from the book of Revelation we know that many likely were—rather, they were motivated by an obligation to follow a certain ethical code.

Tertullian grounds this ethical code in the account of Jesus telling Peter to return his sword to its place, however, other early Church fathers, such as Athenagoras, ground Christian pacifism directly in the teachings found in the Sermon on the Plain (Athenagoras, *A Plea for the Christians*, 11). Clement of Alexandria grounds Christian pacifism on the simple, but profound, commandment of Christ to love (Clement of Alexandria, *the Instructor*, 1.12). If we take the Sermon on the Plain literally, and assume its earliest hearers and readers did the same—it is not surprising that we get the picture of pacifism among the early Christians that we do. These early Christian writers were simply taking Jesus's words at face value.[18] The commandments to "love your enemy" and to "turn the other cheek" completely derail any logic or justification for violence, much less organized military violence.

In fact, so strong was the aversion to military service for many Christians that we have accounts of many Christians preferring the death penalty to military service; such as Maximillian in 295 CE; or Marcellus 3 years later, who actually was a centurion but quit—on pains of death—his service due to his Christian convictions.[19]

These examples tell us that the first Christians took Jesus's ethics and message extremely seriously. The early Christians shaped their lives—communally and individually—according to the ethical teachings of Jesus; even to the point of completely altering their economic relationships. The ethical teachings of Jesus also changed how the early Christians related to wider society, including how they related to the state. Being a Christian in the first few centuries of Christianity cost something, economically, and socially; and for some, it even cost their lives. The commandments of Jesus, no matter how seemingly radical, were not distant ideals for the first Christians; they were commandments to be obeyed, and commandments that they built their lives and communities on.

---

18. Swift, *The Early Fathers on War and Military Service*, 18.
19. Swift, *The Early Fathers on War and Military Service*, 71–75.

Christian Interpretation in late Antiquity

Here we will take a look at a few examples of early Christian interpretations of the Sermon. We will look at Cyril of Alexandria, Basil of Caesarea, Gregory of Nyssa, and John Chrysostom from the east; and Ambrose of Milan, a little bit of Augustine of Hippo, and Pelagius from the west. We will summarize their general approach to the Sermon and then see what we can make of their interpretations. All of the interpreters we will be looking at come from the fourth to the fifth centuries, long after the time of Jesus and the first listeners of the Sermon. We are not looking at the immediate understanding of the Sermon by its intended audience, nor the immediate application of the Sermon by Jesus's followers; rather, we are seeing what Christians were doing with the text in a new context and within a more established Church.

Cyril of Alexandria generally takes a rather literal reading of the text; for example, he interprets the blessings and woes to be a command to embrace poverty (Aquinas, *Catena Aurea 3.1*, 208–209), and a denunciation of the rich (Aquinas, *Catena Aurea 3.1*, 212). He interprets the ethics in a way consistent with his interpretation of the blessings and woes: he claims the generousness and non-violence in the gospels should have concrete results:

> The Lord would moreover have us to be despisers of property.
> (Aquinas, *Catena Aurea 3.1*, 217 [Parker])

He also posits that this ethic will result in being rewarded plentifully by God (Aquinas, *Catena Aurea 3.1*, 223). He reads the parable of the blind leading the blind and the log in the eye parable together. His idea is that Jesus is the teacher, and we the disciples; and that Jesus came not to judge but to show mercy; therefore, if he did not judge, how much less so should we judge, lest we be hypocrites (Aquinas, *Catena Aurea 3.1*, 224).

Basil of Caesarea makes a distinction between the poor who have chosen poverty for the sake of Christ, and those who just happened to be poor, and are not happy about it; the former being the ones that are blessed (Aquinas, *Catena Aurea 3.1*, 208–209). The idea Basil has is that one should practice abstinence of the passions, of materialism, of over eating, of unrestrained expressiveness, and so on and so forth (Aquinas, *Catena Aurea 3.1*, 213–214). Basil takes the admonition to love one's enemy seriously, and all that goes along with it—which includes providing materially for one's enemies—and proclaims that the ethic applies literally, even for, and especially for, government officials and the powerful (Aquinas, *Catena Aurea*

3.1, 215–217). He interprets the lending portion of the ethics as being a strong admonition against usury. He argues that usury is unnatural and covetous, and that the legitimate way to make a living is through labor; for Basil, even begging is better than usury. He claims that the recompense promised in the Sermon, to those who lend without expecting a return, comes from God; since God stands with the poor (Aquinas, *Catena Aurea 3.1,* 221). In his reading of the parables he interprets hypocrisy as a lack of self-knowledge (Aquinas, *Catena Aurea 3.1,* 226).

Ambrose of Milan interprets the blessings and woes as a call to temperance, righteousness, prudence, and fortitude—attaching each of these virtues to each physical state mentioned in the blessings. In this way Ambrose is moralizing and spiritualizing the blessings and woes and taking away their socio-economic significance (Aquinas, *Catena Aurea 3.1,* 208; 211–112). He then takes a rather standard view of the ethics (at least standard for the time)—basically taking them at face value—love those who cause you injury, do not judge, and so on (Aquinas, *Catena Aurea 3.1,* 220–222). He goes on to give an interesting understanding of the parables: interpreting the tree and the fruit parable as a reference to the resurrection to an incorruptible state, the fruit being that state; and the thorns being the condemnation of the flesh (Aquinas, *Catena Aurea 3.1,* 227). In the parable of the houses, he interprets the storm as temptations, heresies, and other spiritual threats (Aquinas, *Catena Aurea 3.1,* 229).

Gregory of Nyssa also makes the blessings and woes about virtue, and spiritualizes them (Aquinas, *Catena Aurea 3.1,* 209–210). Like his brother Basil of Caesarea, he takes Jesus's lending ethics literally and claims that usury is unlawful. He uses rather strong language when speaking on the matter, listing usury with homicide and theft:

> But man ought to shun that baneful anxiety with which he seeks from the poor man increase of his money and gold, exacting a profit of barren metals. Hence he adds, *And lend, hoping for nothing again.* If a man should call the harsh calculation of interest, theft, or homicide, he will not err. For what is the difference, whether a man by digging under a wall become possessed of property, or possess it unlawfully by the compulsory rate of interest? (Aquinas, *Catena Aurea 3.1,* 220–221)

In Pelagius's scathing condemnation of wealth and the rich found in his work *on Riches*[20] he criticizes the spiritual interpretation of the blessings and woes:

> But it is the *evil* rich that he blames,' you will say. Did you then read: Woe to you *evil* that are rich!? Or what need was there to add the label 'rich' at all, if he were not passing his judgement of condemnation upon them because of their riches? If he was rebuking the evil of men specifically, he would simply have said, 'Woe to you that are evil!' And if he is criticising not the rich in general but only the evil that are rich, he ought to have praised the rich that are good, if there are any such men to be found anywhere. And if you want his words, 'Woe to you that are rich!' to refer only to the evil rich, then he ought to say also of the good that are rich, 'Blessed are the rich'.
>
> . . .
>
> At this point I believe you will say, 'He praises the *good* poor'. Why then did he add the label 'poor', if he knew that no special mark of goodness was attached to poverty?
>
> . . .
>
> I wish to add also something that no wise man will be able to dispute, namely, that it is difficult to acquire riches without committing every kind of evil. (Pelagius, *On Riches*, 25–26 [Rees])

Pelagius rules out any attempt to spiritualize the blessings and woes. He does so simply by reading carefully what the text says and taking it at its word. Pelagius here (and in the rest of *On Riches*) is uncompromising in his faithfulness to the teachings of Jesus; he insists on taking them on as they are written, no matter what the implications are, no matter how radical they may seem. When it comes to the blessings and woes his interpretation is clear: wealth is condemned, simply for being wealth; and poverty is praised, simply for being poverty. The reason given for this is that riches are hardly ever acquired without committing every kind of evil. So, for Pelagius, the blessings and woes are not so much eschatological as they are moral.

Pelagius's arch-enemy, Augustine, attempts to cushion the ethics of the Sermon somewhat; for example, when interpreting Jesus's command to give to everyone he writes:

> He says not, To him that seeketh give all things, but give what you justly and honestly can. (Aquinas, *Catena Aurea* 3.1, 217)

---

20. The work *On Riches* or *De Divitiis* was either written by Pelagius himself, or by one of his followers. Bradstock and Rowland, *Radical Christian Writings*, 12.

In this way Augustine tries to make Jesus's words more practical: give what you can, that is enough.

Last but certainly not least, we have John Chrysostom. Chrysostom spiritualizes the blessings and woes, following the trend of many exegetes of the time. For example, he takes the contrast between weeping and laughing in the blessings and woes to mean weeping on behalf of sin rather than laughing (Aquinas, *Catena Aurea 3.1*, 210). The radical nature of Jesus's ethics is not at all lost on Chrysostom, he emphasizes that refraining from hating one's enemy is not enough, but one must love his enemy. His explanation follows his quotation of the text: the enemy should be prayed for and loved because they are "piercing their own souls." He likens the Christian to a physician who might be attacked by a madman, but still shows compassion to that madman and provides him with aid (Aquinas, *Catena Aurea 3.1*, 215–216). An explanation he gives with regards to the commandment to not resist a robber and the commandment to turn the other cheek is that by suffering abuse one puts the abuser to shame; he also appeals to the example of Christ's own suffering to justify our putting up with abuse (Aquinas, *Catena Aurea 3.1*, 217).

Chrysostom's explanation of the economic ethics of the Sermon brings in his own very interesting ethical insights. He says:

> Why (you say) does he not work, why is the idle man fed? Tell me, dost thou then possess by labour? but still if thou workest, dost thou work for this, that thou shouldest blame another? For a single loaf and coat dost thou call a man covetous?
>
> . . .
>
> For if a man is a homicide and a robber, does he not, thinkest thou, deserve to have bread? Let us not then be severe censors of others, lest we too be strictly judged. (Aquinas, *Catena Aurea 3.1*, 217–218)

Chrysostom here gets at the heart of Christian ethics: the obligation one has to another does not depend on any measure of virtue anyone attributes to the other. The fact that one has worked for his bread does not justify not sharing his bread with one who has not, even a murderer or robber deserves bread. In the question about whether one rightfully possesses his property by labor (predicting John Locke's defense of private property) we get an insight into Chrysostom's economic thought. He goes on to say:

> Everything we have we receive from God. But when we speak of "mine and thine," they are only bare words. For if you assert

a house to be yours, you have uttered an expression which wants the substance of reality. For both the air, the soil, and the moisture, are the Creator's. Thou again art he who has built the house; but although the use is thine, it is doubtful, not only because of death, but also on account of the issues of things. Thy soul is not thy own possession, and will be reckoned to thee in like manner as all thy goods. God wishes those things to be thine which are entrusted to thee for thy brethren, and they will be thine if thou hast dispensed them for others. But if thou hast spent richly upon thyself what things are thine, they are now become another's. (Aquinas, *Catena Aurea 3.1*, 218)

This is a great summation of the Christian ethic as it would be applied to economics: what you claim is yours, is really God's; and God wishes everything to be shared. Thus, when Jesus commands to give to anyone who asks, he means it. Similarly, when it comes to lending, he says:

Observe the wonderful nature of lending, one receives and another binds himself for his debts, giving a hundred fold at the present time, and in the future eternal life. (Aquinas, *Catena Aurea 3.1*, 221)

This is a beautiful observation by Chrysostom, and a factual one. Lending—when done without economic calculation—binds people together. Ultimately, Chrysostom sees the economic imperative to share and lend as being grounded in theology: all things are God's, and he desires us to share; and our reward from God depends on our obedience to God's desire for us. Chrysostom most certainly understands that the ethics of the Sermon on the Plain are no exaggeration, he makes it very clear that he believes Jesus meant what he said (Aquinas, *Catena Aurea 3.1*, 219). He demonstrates this by some examples. One being that of Paul, who did good to those that stoned him; and he claims that the love one is to have for one's enemies is a spiritual love—a love that goes beyond the natural and beyond what is common—but a love with absolutely concrete consequences in the real world (Aquinas, *Catena Aurea 3.1*, 219-220). In his reading of the command to not judge, he takes a very practical interpretation: if someone is going on the wrong path, reacting with love will help them more than judgement will (Aquinas, *Catena Aurea 3.1*, 222).

What we see in this small sample of early interpretations of the text is a wide variety of readings, most taking the blessings and woes spiritually. This spiritualization is understandable given the parallel blessings of Matthew as well as the obvious fact that there were pious Christians of considerable wealth in late antiquity. Two exegetes of those whom we have sampled do not spiritualize the blessings and woes: Cyril of Alexandria and Pelagius. Cyril of Alexandria interprets them as calling people to individual voluntary poverty; not as an eschatological social vision. Pelagius interprets them as simply a straight up condemnation of riches and a praise of poverty; the reason given is that the acquiring of riches involves sin. The real split, however, comes when we arrive at the ethics. Most of the eastern interpreters take the ethics literally and take them on completely—with all their radical implications and commandments—even to the point of drawing out socio-political implications; such as the banning of usury, a condemnation of private property, and a denunciation of retributive justice by the state. Some of the western interpreters tend to try to dampen, or qualify, the ethical commandments found in the Sermon. This is especially the case with Augustine of Hippo who goes out of his way to try and make Jesus's commandments "realistic," at least realistic within the socio-economic/political framework that Augustine found himself in. For Augustine, the ideal must be qualified by the reality on the ground, and the application must be reasonable given the current circumstances.

The reason I have laid out a quick sketch of some interpretations of the Sermon is that it can be enlightening to see how Christianity developed outside of the context from which it was birthed; as well as to see how it developed in to the forms of Christianity we see today. The Sermon on the Plain, with its relentlessly demanding ethic, gives a large and tempting incentive to interpreters to limit its scope, to spiritualize it, or to dampen its demands. We see bits of that in the fourth and fifth century. But we also see interpreters reading the text, being confronted by its demands and implications, and—because of their strong faith and piety—attempting to remain faithful to the text and go to the very end with it. John Chrysostom's admission that the very nature of property is put into question by the ethics, and Basil of Caesarea's admission that the demand to love one's enemy would apply even to government officials, shows that many of these early interpreters took the ethics absolutely seriously.

7

An Eschatological Community

JESUS'S ETHIC OF ABSOLUTE unselfish love, and his ethics of sharing and non-violence can be seen by many as unrealistic. Some may consider that the Sermon demands some kind of absolute giving of one's self, and wonder if such a stance is possible; they may even question the possibility of a non-quid pro quo relationship entirely. Some philosophers have questioned whether there can be such a thing as a true gift, and this doubt often begins with an idea of a gift being a one-way transaction. For example, Jaquess Derrida writes:

> For there to be a gift, there must be no reciprocity, return, exchange, countergift, or debt.[1]

Later on, he writes:

> It is thus necessary, at the limit, that he does not recognize the gift as a gift. If he recognizes it as a gift, if the gift appears to him as such, if the present is present to him as a present, this simple recognition suffices to annul the gift. Why? Because it gives back, in the place, let us say, of the thing itself, a symbolic equivalent.
>
> . . .
>
> The symbolic opens and constitutes the order of exchange and of debt, the law or the order of circulation in which the gift gets annulled.[2]

Basically, the argument here is that the giver of something is engaging in exchange—and thus not giving a true gift—if he gets anything back, or if he

1. Derrida, "The Time of the King," in Schrift, *The logic of the gift*, 128.
2. Derrida, "The Time of the King," in Schrift, *The logic of the gift*, 129.

is owed anything back, even if what he is owed or given back is only recognition that he has given a gift. The assumption here is that your two options are absolute one-sided giving, or exchange. According to Derrida, society is a system of exchanges, and a gift, is an attempt, to escape that system. On the role of exchange in society anthropologist Levi-Strauss wrote:

> Exchanges are peacefully resolved wars and wars are the result of unsuccessful transactions.[3]

Jesus's ethics are the ethics of love, and these ethics undercut Derrida's idea of the dichotomy between "gift" and "exchange," and they also give us an alternative to Levi-Strauss's "war or exchange" dichotomy. Jesus's ethics also undercut the basis of Hobbes's and Locke's social contract theory; both of which depend on an atomized view of the human in the state of nature. In Hobbes's case, this state of nature is brutality and violent struggle for superiority;[4] in Locke's case, it is the individual with his or her rights.[5]

We can undercut Derrida's dichotomy by simply doing a quick phenomenology of a specific kind of love: romantic love. When a man loves a woman and does something as simple as making her a nice romantic dinner, there must be a return, in the sense of the woman feeling happy, feeling loved, feeling appreciated. This return results in the man knowing that he is the cause of those feelings which results in him feeling happy himself. Yet we would not say that this man is engaging in an exchange relationship, why? Because there is nothing resembling a contract going on, nor is there any debt being accrued. In fact, if the woman treated it as though it were a contract—or acted in a way that would imply that her reciprocity was the result of some debt accrued by the dinner—the man would feel as though the dinner had failed and that the love they shared was in jeopardy. Yet at the same time, if the woman ate the dinner and left, treating the dinner as simply something she had received, the man would also feel as though the dinner had failed. This kind of situation is not unique to romantic love, it is experienced in friendships, among strangers, in families, among neighbors, and so on to varying degrees. This is because, ultimately, the entire exercise is not primarily about the providing of a meal and the receipt of appreciation; it is about the relationship between the man and the woman.

---

3. Levi-Strauss, *The Elementary structures of Kinship*, 67.

4. See Thomas Hobbes, *Leviathan.*

5. See John Locke, *Second Treatise of Government.*

The meal is a means to the end of building the relationship.[6] The meal must be understood within the context of the communal realm, not any market or market like realm.[7]

This is why Jesus can both seem to be extreme in his social ethics—lending without expecting return, loving enemies, giving to all, refraining from retaliation and so on—while at the same time be absolutely committed to the normative nature of those ethics. It is because he is making love the central organizing principle.

The concept of love can be somewhat vague, so let us try and pin it down. Philosopher Alain Badiou defines love this way:

> My own philosophical view is attempting to say that love cannot be reduced to any of these approximations and is a quest for truth. What kind of truth? You will ask. I mean truth in relation to something quite precise: what kind of world does one see when one experiences it from the point of view of two and not one? What is the world like when it is experienced, developed and lived from the point of view of difference and not identity? That is what I believe love to be.[8]

Another philosopher who tries to define love is Simon May. May defines love this way:

> Love is the rapture we feel for people who (or things that) inspire in us the experience or hope of ontological rootedness—a rapture that triggers and sustains the long search for a vital relationship between our being and theirs. We experience their mere presence as grounding—or as a promise of grounding—because it seems to be receptive to, to recognize, to echo, to provide a powerful berth to, what we regard as most essential about us.[9]

These two definitions both capture aspects of love that we understand intuitively: to love someone is to build a world with that person, to experience the world as a "we;" it is also a grounding of our being, we root ourselves in a person and tie our being to that person. Jesus, in the Sermon—or in the Synoptics in general—never really gives a concrete definition of love, although from the Sermon we can know that it has something to do with an idea of unmeasured giving and surrender. In the Johannian literature

---

6. Eagleton, *Radical Sacrifice*, 116.

7. Gudeman, *The Anthropology of the Economy*, 10.

8. Badiou, *In Praise of Love*, 22.

9. May, *Love*, 240.

however, we have a somewhat more developed concept of love. In the Gospel of John, we read:

> "This is my commandment, that you love one another as I have loved you. No one has greater love than this, to lay down one's life for one's friends. You are my friends if you do what I command you. (John 15:12–14)

We can understand a few things about John's representation of Jesus's concept of love. First of all, we see that love is something which Jesus commands. Love as a commandment goes against the intuition of thinking of love as a spontaneous emotion, but it is in line with the notion of love given by the two philosophers Alain Badiou and Simon May mentioned above. It is perfectly possible to command someone to engage in a project of constructing a world from the standpoint of "we" rather than "I," it is also perfectly possible to command someone to ground his being in something. A second thing we understand from these verses is that Jesus's concept of love (as represented by John) is exemplified in the way Jesus loved his disciples. The main aspect of Jesus's exemplification of love seems to be the "laying down of one's life for his friends." Clearly what John is communicating here is that the death of Jesus is the model of love. This is not exactly compatible with Alain Badiou's or Simon May's concepts of love. If the greatest form of love is self-sacrifice for one's friend, then that kind of love cannot build a world from the point of view of two (or more) and not one, since one party is sacrificing himself; neither can it be a form of grounding one's being, quite the opposite actually.

Before we examine this conflict, let us look at two passages in 1 John that will both clarify and complicate our picture of John's concept of love. The first says:

> For this is the message you have heard from the beginning, that we should love one another. We must not be like Cain who was from the evil one and murdered his brother. And why did he murder him? Because his own deeds were evil and his brother's righteous. Do not be astonished, brothers and sisters, that the world hates you. We know that we have passed from death to life because we love one another. Whoever does not love abides in death. All who hate a brother or sister are murderers, and you know that murderers do not have eternal life abiding in them. We know love by this, that he laid down his life for us—and we ought to lay down our lives for one another. How does God's love abide in anyone who has the world's goods and sees a brother or sister in need and

yet refuses help? Little children, let us love, not in word or speech, but in truth and action. (1 John 3:11–18)

The second:

Beloved, let us love one another, because love is from God; everyone who loves is born of God and knows God. Whoever does not love does not know God, for God is love. God's love was revealed among us in this way: God sent his only Son into the world so that we might live through him. In this is love, not that we loved God but that he loved us and sent his Son to be the atoning sacrifice for our sins. Beloved, since God loved us so much, we also ought to love one another. No one has ever seen God; if we love one another, God lives in us, and his love is perfected in us. (1 John 4:7–12)

From these verses we see that John's definition of love is applied to all of Jesus's disciples, all are to lay their lives down for their friends, or at least be willing to. We also see that this willingness should manifest itself in concrete acts of mutual aid, especially to those in need. Looking at the commandment from this context we see it somewhat simplified: self-sacrifice is the maximum command, you have to be willing to give your life; but in everyday interactions it should lead to self-sacrificial mutual aid for those who are in need.

We also see that God himself is defined as love, and that the only way to know God is to love; and that this love—which is God, and is revealed in Christ's sacrifice—can only be known through the act of loving one another. This somewhat complicates issues in that love is not only defined as ultimate sacrifice but as God himself. Without getting too theological, I would like to suggest that perhaps God as creator and redeemer—i.e. the giver of not only existence itself but also the means of reconciliation between the given and the giver (Creation and God)—is the sense in which John can say "God is love," and that this love is the same love defined as self-sacrifice. God is God because of his love, his creation, revelation, and reconciliation—outside of which God is undefinable—therefore, John can honestly and literally say that "God is love." The giving of his son—which John says reveals God—is a gift of sacrifice that is done for the sake of reconciliation, for the sake of bringing God and creation back into communion, or a sharing of mutual enjoyment.

Returning to the conflict between the idea of love as self-sacrifice, Alain Badiou's notion of love as the creation of a "we" point of view, and Simon May's notion of love as grounding—we can perhaps reconcile the concepts somewhat by bringing God into the picture. John, in his first *epistle*, makes it very clear that one's relationship with God is dependent on one's relationship with his fellow. So, by loving our fellow to the point of death we are both creating a "we," and grounding our being; not necessarily with our fellow alone, but also with God; so that even if we die, that "we" and that grounding is not dissolved. This of course depends on the belief in a general resurrection, which was the belief of Jesus, much of first-century Judaism, and the earliest Christians.

Bringing this back to the Sermon on the Plain, we can understand both the seemingly extreme demands of Jesus (loving enemies, giving to all, lending without expecting return, never retaliating, and so on), as well as the being "sons of the Most High" by meeting those demands, much better through John's definition of love. If love is self-sacrifice up to the point of death—for the sake of reconciliation and communion—then an ethical system built around love would be one of extreme self-giving leading to communion, which would be the opposite of reciprocal exchange which is giving and receiving in a manner that does not necessitate communion but in fact dissolves it. To clarify the difference between giving and receiving in a way that does not necessitate communion as opposed to giving and receiving in a way that does, let us look at David Graeber's explanation of exchange as opposed to communism. Discussing exchange, David Graeber writes:

> Exchange allows us to cancel out our debts. It gives us a way to call it even: hence, to end the relationship. With vendors, one is usually only pretending to have a relationship at all.[10]

As opposed to communism:

> unlike what happens in communism, which always partakes of a certain notion of eternity, the entire relationship [that of exchange] can be canceled out, and either party can call an end to it at any time.[11]

Derrida questioned whether a true gift was possible—defined as a purely one-sided transfer— self-sacrifice however, does not concern itself with the return; it concerns itself with the giving up of one's self for the other so that communion can take place. It is the communion that is important, not what is given or received. In other words, the ethic of love moves all of

10. Graeber, *Debt,* 104.

11. Graeber, *Debt,* 103.

life into the communal realm, even to the point of including one's enemies and debtors within one's communal realm. Of course, this is no mere secular revolutionary ethic; as Jesus points out from the blessings and woes, this is entirely based on the *eschaton*, when God establishes his kingdom and reverses the social structure. In Jesus's ethics, the moving of human relationships into the communal realm is done in light of the Kingdom of God, where God will be in communion with humankind. Man's sharing is grounded in God's giving. The ethics of community are grounded ultimately in God's teleology. Terry Eagleton puts it this way:

> Yet though God has no need of a return from his creatures, his grace lies at the source of their own giving and gratitude. In this sense, exchange and gratuitousness, the reciprocal and the unilateral, are not incompatible.[12]

The Sermon on the Plain, Jesus's manifesto, is a manifesto to establish an eschatological community, a community of love and mutual aid on the side of the eschatological Kingdom of God.

12. Eagleton, *Radical Sacrifice*, 114.

The Sermon on the Plain and Translation

THE TRANSLATION OF THE Sermon on the Plain which I use throughout this book is my own. I have produced by own translation because—for the sake of the purpose of this book—I wanted a very literal translation that retains, as much as possible, the original structure and vocabulary of the Greek. This translation will, in some places, seem a little awkward, this is because I have not smoothed out the grammar in order to render it into good English; rather, I have kept everything as literal as possible while attempting to render it readable in English. Of course, no translation is perfect, and all translations necessarily add a layer of interpretation, however, I hope that mine is useful in that it allows for a more detailed analysis of the text. The Greek text of the Sermon is from the Nestle-Aland Novum Testamentum Graece 28th revised edition. Single brackets surrounding words (in both the Greek and English text) indicate that textual critics today are not completely convinced of the authenticity of the enclosed words. Double brackets surrounding words (in the English text) are words which are not in the original Greek, but which I have nevertheless added in order to retain the meaning of the Greek text in English. The second person pronoun in all capital letters in the English text is used to translate second personal plural pronouns in the Greek text. The Sermon on the Plain (Luke 6:20–49):

Καὶ αὐτὸς ἐπάρας τοὺς ὀφθαλμοὺς αὐτοῦ εἰς τοὺς μαθητὰς αὐτοῦ ἔλεγεν·

And having raised his eyes to his disciples he said:

Μακάριοι οἱ πτωχοί, ὅτι ὑμετέρα ἐστὶν ἡ βασιλεία τοῦ θεοῦ.

How happy are the destitute, because the Kingdom of God is YOURS.

μακάριοι οἱ πεινῶντες νῦν, ὅτι χορτασθήσεσθε.

How happy are the ones hungering now, because YOU will be made full.

μακάριοι οἱ κλαίοντες νῦν, ὅτι γελάσετε.

How happy are the ones weeping now, because YOU will laugh.

μακάριοί ἐστε ὅταν μισήσωσιν ὑμᾶς οἱ ἄνθρωποι καὶ ὅταν ἀφορίσωσιν ὑμᾶς καὶ ὀνειδίσωσιν καὶ ἐκβάλωσιν τὸ ὄνομα ὑμῶν ὡς πονηρὸν ἕνεκα τοῦ υἱοῦ τοῦ ἀνθρώπου·

How happy YOU are whenever people hate YOU, and when they separate from YOU, and when they revile YOU and cast out YOUR name as wicked on account of the Son of Man.

χάρητε ἐν ἐκείνῃ τῇ ἡμέρᾳ καὶ σκιρτήσατε, ἰδοὺ γὰρ ὁ μισθὸς ὑμῶν πολὺς ἐν τῷ οὐρανῷ· κατὰ τὰ αὐτὰ γὰρ ἐποίουν τοῖς προφήταις οἱ πατέρες αὐτῶν.

Rejoice in that day and leap for joy, because look, YOUR reward in heaven is great—for their fathers were doing these things against the prophets.

Πλὴν οὐαὶ ὑμῖν τοῖς πλουσίοις, ὅτι ἀπέχετε τὴν παράκλησιν ὑμῶν.

Nevertheless, Woe to YOU, the rich, because YOU are receiving YOUR comfort.

οὐαὶ ὑμῖν, οἱ ἐμπεπλησμένοι νῦν, ὅτι πεινάσετε.

Woe to YOU, the ones who have been filled now; because YOU will hunger.

οὐαί, οἱ γελῶντες νῦν, ὅτι πενθήσετε καὶ κλαύσετε.

Woe to the ones laughing now, because YOU will mourn and weep.

οὐαὶ ὅταν ὑμᾶς καλῶς εἴπωσιν πάντες οἱ ἄνθρωποι· κατὰ τὰ αὐτὰ γὰρ ἐποίουν τοῖς ψευδοπροφήταις οἱ πατέρες αὐτῶν.

Woe when all people may speak well of YOU, because their fathers were doing these things to the false prophets.

Ἀλλ᾽ ὑμῖν λέγω τοῖς ἀκούουσιν· ἀγαπᾶτε τοὺς ἐχθροὺς ὑμῶν, καλῶς ποιεῖτε τοῖς μισοῦσιν ὑμᾶς,

But to YOU, to those listening, I say—love YOUR enemy, do good to those hating YOU.

εὐλογεῖτε τοὺς καταρωμένους ὑμᾶς, προσεύχεσθε περὶ τῶν ἐπηρεαζόντων ὑμᾶς.

Bless those cursing YOU, pray for those who insult YOU.

τῷ τύπτοντί σε ἐπὶ τὴν σιαγόνα πάρεχε καὶ τὴν ἄλλην, καὶ ἀπὸ τοῦ αἴροντός σου τὸ ἱμάτιον καὶ τὸν χιτῶνα μὴ κωλύσῃς.

To the one striking you on the cheek, offer also the other; and from the one taking your coat, do not hold back even your tunic.

Παντὶ αἰτοῦντί σε δίδου, καὶ ἀπὸ τοῦ αἴροντος τὰ σὰ μὴ ἀπαίτει.

Give to all that request of you; and from the one taking from you, do not demand it back.

Καὶ καθὼς θέλετε ἵνα ποιῶσιν ὑμῖν οἱ ἄνθρωποι ποιεῖτε αὐτοῖς ὁμοίως.

And just as YOU want people to do to YOU, YOU do likewise.

καὶ εἰ ἀγαπᾶτε τοὺς ἀγαπῶντας ὑμᾶς, ποία ὑμῖν χάρις ἐστίν; καὶ γὰρ οἱ ἁμαρτωλοὶ τοὺς ἀγαπῶντας αὐτοὺς ἀγαπῶσιν.

And if YOU love those loving YOU, what credit is it to YOU? For also the sinners love the ones loving them.

καὶ [γὰρ] ἐὰν ἀγαθοποιῆτε τοὺς ἀγαθοποιοῦντας ὑμᾶς, ποία ὑμῖν χάρις ἐστίν; καὶ οἱ ἁμαρτωλοὶ τὸ αὐτὸ ποιοῦσιν.

[For] Also if YOU do good to those doing good to YOU, what credit is it to YOU? The sinners also do it.

καὶ ἐὰν δανίσητε παρ᾽ ὧν ἐλπίζετε λαβεῖν, ποία ὑμῖν χάρις [ἐστίν]; καὶ ἁμαρτωλοὶ ἁμαρτωλοῖς δανίζουσιν ἵνα ἀπολάβωσιν τὰ ἴσα.

And if YOU lend to those from whom YOU hope to receive, what credit [is] it] to YOU? Sinners also lend to sinners in order that they might get back the same.

πλὴν ἀγαπᾶτε τοὺς ἐχθροὺς ὑμῶν καὶ ἀγαθοποιεῖτε καὶ δανίζετε μηδὲν ἀπελπίζοντες· καὶ ἔσται ὁ μισθὸς ὑμῶν πολύς, καὶ ἔσεσθε υἱοὶ ὑψίστου, ὅτι αὐτὸς χρηστός ἐστιν ἐπὶ τοὺς ἀχαρίστους καὶ πονηρούς.

Nevertheless, love YOUR enemies, and do good and lend expecting nothing in return, and YOUR reward will be great, and YOU will be sons of the Most High—because he is gracious upon the ungrateful and wicked.

Γίνεσθε οἰκτίρμονες καθὼς [καὶ] ὁ πατὴρ ὑμῶν οἰκτίρμων ἐστίν.

Become merciful just as YOUR father is [also] merciful to YOU.

Καὶ μὴ κρίνετε, καὶ οὐ μὴ κριθῆτε· καὶ μὴ καταδικάζετε, καὶ οὐ μὴ καταδικασθῆτε. ἀπολύετε, καὶ ἀπολυθήσεσθε·

Also do not judge, and YOU will not be judged; and do not condemn, and YOU will not be condemned; release, and YOU will be released,

δίδοτε, καὶ δοθήσεται ὑμῖν· μέτρον καλὸν πεπιεσμένον σεσαλευμένον ὑπερεκχυννόμενον δώσουσιν εἰς τὸν κόλπον ὑμῶν· ᾧ γὰρ μέτρῳ μετρεῖτε ἀντιμετρηθήσεται ὑμῖν.

give, and it will be given to YOU, they will give a good measure, pressed down, shaken, overflowing in YOUR bosom—for that measure YOU measure out, it will be measured in return to YOU.

Εἶπεν δὲ καὶ παραβολὴν αὐτοῖς· μήτι δύναται τυφλὸς τυφλὸν ὁδηγεῖν; οὐχὶ ἀμφότεροι εἰς βόθυνον ἐμπεσοῦνται;

Then he also spoke a parable to them, a blind man is not able to guide a blind man, is he? Will not both of them fall into a pit?

οὐκ ἔστιν μαθητὴς ὑπὲρ τὸν διδάσκαλον· κατηρτισμένος δὲ πᾶς ἔσται ὡς ὁ διδάσκαλος αὐτοῦ.

A disciple is not above the teacher, but everyone being fully qualified will be as his teacher.

Τί δὲ βλέπεις τὸ κάρφος τὸ ἐν τῷ ὀφθαλμῷ τοῦ ἀδελφοῦ σου, τὴν δὲ δοκὸν τὴν ἐν τῷ ἰδίῳ ὀφθαλμῷ οὐ κατανοεῖς;

Why do you see the speck in your brother's eye, but the beam in your own eye you do not consider?

πῶς δύνασαι λέγειν τῷ ἀδελφῷ σου· ἀδελφέ, ἄφες ἐκβάλω τὸ κάρφος τὸ ἐν τῷ ὀφθαλμῷ σου, αὐτὸς τὴν ἐν τῷ ὀφθαλμῷ σου δοκὸν οὐ βλέπων; ὑποκριτά, ἔκβαλε πρῶτον τὴν δοκὸν ἐκ τοῦ ὀφθαλμοῦ σου, καὶ τότε διαβλέψεις τὸ κάρφος τὸ ἐν τῷ ὀφθαλμῷ τοῦ ἀδελφοῦ σου ἐκβαλεῖν.

How are you able to say to your brother "brother, allow me to get out the speck in your eye," while you yourself are not seeing the beam in your eye. Hypocrite, first get the beam out from your eye, and then you will see clearly to get out the speck in your brother's eye.

Οὐ γάρ ἐστιν δένδρον καλὸν ποιοῦν καρπὸν σαπρόν, οὐδὲ πάλιν δένδρον σαπρὸν ποιοῦν καρπὸν καλόν.

For no fine tree is producing rotten fruit; on the other hand, nor does a rotten tree produce fine fruit.

ἕκαστον γὰρ δένδρον ἐκ τοῦ ἰδίου καρποῦ γινώσκεται· οὐ γὰρ ἐξ ἀκανθῶν συλλέγουσιν σῦκα οὐδὲ ἐκ βάτου σταφυλὴν τρυγῶσιν.

For each tree is known from its own fruit—because they do not gather figs from thorns, neither do they cut grapes from thorn-bushes.

ὁ ἀγαθὸς ἄνθρωπος ἐκ τοῦ ἀγαθοῦ θησαυροῦ τῆς καρδίας προφέρει τὸ ἀγαθόν, καὶ ὁ πονηρὸς ἐκ τοῦ πονηροῦ προφέρει τὸ πονηρόν· ἐκ γὰρ περισσεύματος καρδίας λαλεῖ τὸ στόμα αὐτοῦ.

A good person brings forth good from the good treasure from his heart, and the wicked brings forth wickedness from his wicked [[heart]]—for out of the abundance of his heart his mouth speaks.

Τί δέ με καλεῖτε· κύριε κύριε, καὶ οὐ ποιεῖτε ἃ λέγω;

But why do YOU call me "lord lord," and YOU do not do what I say;

Πᾶς ὁ ἐρχόμενος πρός με καὶ ἀκούων μου τῶν λόγων καὶ ποιῶν αὐτούς, ὑποδείξω ὑμῖν τίνι ἐστὶν ὅμοιος·

Everyone coming to me and hearing my words and doing them—I will show YOU whom he is like—

ὅμοιός ἐστιν ἀνθρώπῳ οἰκοδομοῦντι οἰκίαν ὃς ἔσκαψεν καὶ ἐβάθυνεν καὶ ἔθηκεν θεμέλιον ἐπὶ τὴν πέτραν· πλημμύρης δὲ γενομένης προσέρηξεν ὁ ποταμὸς τῇ οἰκίᾳ ἐκείνῃ, καὶ οὐκ ἴσχυσεν σαλεῦσαι αὐτὴν διὰ τὸ καλῶς οἰκοδομῆσθαι αὐτήν.

he is like a man building up a house who dug and went deep and laid a foundation upon the rock. But with the coming of the flood, the river bursts against that house; and was not able to shake it due to its having been built well.

ὁ δὲ ἀκούσας καὶ μὴ ποιήσας ὅμοιός ἐστιν ἀνθρώπῳ οἰκοδομήσαντι οἰκίαν ἐπὶ τὴν γῆν χωρὶς θεμελίου, ᾗ προσέρηξεν ὁ ποταμός, καὶ εὐθὺς συνέπεσεν καὶ ἐγένετο τὸ ῥῆγμα τῆς οἰκίας ἐκείνης μέγα.

But the one having heard and not doing is like a man that having built up a house upon the ground without a foundation, which the river burst against, and it immediately collapsed, and the ruin of that house came to be great.

Bibliography

"A Messianic Apocalypse." Translated by Geza Vermes. In *The Complete Dead Sea Scrolls in English*, Geza Vermes. London: Penguin Classics, 2004.

"Aboth." Translated by Herbert Danby. *The Mishnah: Translated from the Hebrew with Introduction and Brief Explanatory Notes,* edited by Herbert Danby. Peabody: Hendricksons, 2013.

"Arachin." In *The William Davidson digital edition of the Koren Noé Talmud, with commentary by Rabbi Adin Steinsaltz Even-Israel.* New York: Sefaria, 2017.

"Baba Bathra." In *The William Davidson digital edition of the Koren Noé Talmud, with commentary by Rabbi Adin Steinsaltz Even-Israel.* New York: Sefaria, 2017.

"Babba Kamma." Translated by Herbert Danby. *The Mishnah: Translated from the Hebrew with Introduction and Brief Explanatory Notes,* edited by Herbert Danby. Peabody: Hendricksons, 2013.

"Babba Kamma." In *The William Davidson digital edition of the Koren Noé Talmud, with commentary by Rabbi Adin Steinsaltz Even-Israel.* New York: Sefaria, 2017.

"Babba Metzia." Translated by Herbert Danby. *The Mishnah: Translated from the Hebrew with Introduction and Brief Explanatory Notes,* edited by Herbert Danby. Peabody: Hendricksons, 2013.

"Book of Enoch." Translated by E. Isaac. In *The Old Testament Pseudepigrapha: Apocalyptic Literature and Testaments*, edited by James H. Charlesworth. New York: Doubleday & Company, 1983.

"Commentary on Psalms." Translated by Geza Vermes. In *The Complete Dead Sea Scrolls in English,* Geza Vermes. London: Penguin Classics, 2004.

"First Clement." In *The Apostolic Fathers in English.* Translated by Michael W. Holmes. Grand Rapids: Baker Academic, 2006.

"Gospel of Thomas." Translated by Stephen Patterson and Marvin Meyer. In *The Complete Gospels: Annotated Scholars Version.* San Francisco: HarperOne, 1994.

"Kiddushin." Translated by Herbert Danby. *The Mishnah: Translated from the Hebrew with Introduction and Brief Explanatory Notes,* edited by Herbert Danby. Peabody: Hendricksons, 2013.

"Psalms of Solomon." Introduction by R.B. Wright. In *The Old Testament Pseudepigrapha: Expansions of the "Old Testament" and Legends, Wisdom and Philosophical Literature, Prayers, Psalms and Odes, Fragments of lost Judeo-Hellenistic Works,* edited by James H. Charlesworth. New York: Doubleday & Company, 1985.

"Sabbath." In *The William Davidson digital edition of the Koren Noé Talmud, with commentary by Rabbi Adin Steinsaltz Even-Israel.* New York: Sefaria, 2017.

"Shebiith." Translated by Herbert Danby. *The Mishnah: Translated from the Hebrew with Introduction and Brief Explanatory Notes,* Herbert Danby. Peabody: Hendricksons, 2013.

"The Apocalypse of 2 Enoch." Translated by F. I. Andersen. In *The Old Testament Pseudepigrapha: Apocalyptic Literature and Testaments,* edited by James H. Charlesworth. New York: Doubleday & Company, 1983.

"The Community Rule." Translated by Geza Vermes. In *The Complete Dead Sea Scrolls in English,* Geza Vermes. London: Penguin Classics, 2004.

"The Damascus Document." Translated by Geza Vermes. In *The Complete Dead Sea Scrolls in English,* Geza Vermes. London: Penguin Classics, 2004.

"The Didache." In *The Apostolic Fathers in English.* Translated by Michael W. Holmes. Grand Rapids: Baker Academic, 2006.

"The Heavenly Prince Melchizedek." Translated by Geza Vermes. In *The Complete Dead Sea Scrolls in English,* Geza Vermes. London: Penguin Classics, 2004.

"The Letter of Polycarp to the Philippians." In *The Apostolic Fathers in English,* Translated by Michael W. Holmes. Grand Rapids: Baker Academic, 2006.

"The Thanksgiving Hymns." Translated by Geza Vermes. In *The Complete Dead Sea Scrolls in English,* Geza Vermes. London: Penguin Classics, 2004.

"The War Scroll." Translated by Geza Vermes. In *The Complete Dead Sea Scrolls in English,* Geza Vermes. London: Penguin Classics, 2004.

Allison, Dale. *Constructing Jesus: Memory, Imagination, and History.* Grand Rapids: Baker Academic, 2010.

Aquinas, Thomas. *St. Luke: Vol 1.* Catena Aurea: Commentary on the Four Gospels collected out of the Works of the Fathers. Translated by John Henry Parker. London: James Parker and Company, 1874.

Aristotle. *The Nicomachean Ethics.* Translated by William David Ross. Oxford: Clarendon, 1908.

Arnal, William E. "Why Q Failed." In *Redescribing Christian Origins,* edited by Christopher R. Matthews. Atlanta: SBL Press, 2004.

Athenagoras. "A Plea for the Christians." Translated by B.P. Pratten. In *Ante-Nicene Fathers. Vol. 2,* edited by Alexander Roberts, James Donaldson, and A. Cleveland Coxe. Buffalo: Christian Literature Publishing Company, 1885.

Aviam, Mordechai. "People, Land, Economy and Belief in First-Century Galilee and its Origins: A Comprehensive Archaeological Synthesis." In *The Galilean Economy in the time of Jesus,* edited by David A. Fiensy and Ralph K. Hawkins. Atlanta: SBL Press, 2013.

Badiou, Alain. *In Praise of Love.* Translated by Nicolas Truong. London: Serpent's Tail, 2012.

Bauer, W., F. W. Danker, W. F. Arndt, and F. W. Gingrich. *Greek-English Lexicon of the New Testament and Other Early Christian Literature. 3d ed.* Chicago: University of Chicago Press, 1999.

Bellinzoni, Arthur J. "The Gospel of Luke in the Apostolic Fathers: An Overview." *Trajectories through the New Testament and the Apostolic Fathers,* edited by Andrew F. Gregory and Christopher M. Tuckett. Oxford: Oxford University Press, 2005.

Betz, Hans Dieter. *A commentary on the Sermon on the Mount, including the Sermon on the Plain.* Hermeneia: A Critical and Historical Commentary on the Bible. Minneapolis: Fortress, 1995.

Bock, Darrell L. *The Theology of Luke and Acts*. Biblical Theology of the New Testament Series. Grand Rapids: Zondervan, 2012.

Bradstock, Andrew and Rowland, Christopher. *Radical Christian Writings: A reader*. Hoboken: Wiley-Blackwell, 2002.

Cicero. *De Finibus*. Translated by H. Rackham. Loeb Classical Library. Cambridge: Harvard University Press, 1914.

Clement of Alexandria. "The Instructor." Translated by William Wilson. In *Ante-Nicene Christian Library Vol. 2*, edited by Alexander Roberts, James Donaldson, and A. Cleveland Coxe. Buffalo: Christian Literature Publishing Company, 1885.

Colish, Marcia L. *The Stoic Tradition: From Antiquity to the Early Middle Ages*. Leiden: Brill, 1985.

Crossley, James G. *Why Christianity Happened: A Sociohistorical Account of Christian Origins (26–50ce)*. Louisville: Westminster John Knox, 2006.

Derrenbacker, Robert A. "Ancient Compositional Practices and the Synoptic Problem." Phd Diss., University of St. Michael's College, 2001.

Derrida, Jacques. "The Time of the King." In *The logic of the gift*, edited by Alan D. Schrift. New York: Routledge, 1997.

Dihle, Albrecht. *Goldene Regel: Eine Einführung in die Geschichte der antiken und frühchristlichen Vulgärethik*. Göttingen: Vandenhoeck & Ruprecht, 1962.

Diogenes Laertius. *Lives of the Eminent Philosophers Vol. 1*. Translated by Robert Drew. Loeb Classical Library. Cambridge: Harvard University Press, 1925.

Dunn, James D. *Jesus Remembered: Christianity in the Making Vol. 1*. Grand Rapids: Eerdmans, 2003.

Eagleton, Terry. *Radical Sacrifice*. New Haven: Yale University Press, 2018.

Edwards Douglas. "The Socio-Economic and Cultural Ethos of Lower Galilee in the First Century: Implications for the Nascent Jesus Movement." In *The Galilee in Late Antiquity*, edited by Lee I. Levine. New York: The Jewish Theological Seminary of America, 1994.

Epictetus. *Discourses: Books III–IV, The Encheiridion*. Translated by William Abbot Oldfather. Loeb Classical Library. Cambridge: Harvard University Press, 1928.

Epicurus. *Letters, Principle Doctrines, and Vatican Sayings*. Translated by Russel Geer. London: Pearson, 1964.

Eusebius of Caesarea. "Church History." Translated by Arthur Cushman McGiffer. In *Nicene and Post-Nicene Fathers, Second Series Vol. 1*, edited by Philip Schaff and Henry Wace. Buffalo, NY: Christian Literature Publishing Co., 1890.

——— *Praeparatio Evangelica*. Translated by E.H. Gifford. Oxford: Oxford Univeristy Press, 1903.

Evans, C.F. *Saint Luke*. London: SCM Press, 2008.

Ferguson Everett. *Backgrounds of Early Christianity*. Grand Rapids: Eerdmans, 2003.

Fiske, Alan. *Structures of Social Life*. New York: Free Press, 1993.

Fitzmyer, J.A. *The Gospel According to Luke I–IX*. Anchor Bible Commentaries. New Haven: Yale University Press, 2017.

Freuchen, Peter, *Book of the Eskimos*, Cleveland: World Publishing Company, 1961.

Freyne, Sean. "Galilee and Judea in the first century." In *The Cambridge History of Christianity: Christianity, Origins to Constantine*, edited by Margaret M. Mitchell and Frances M. Young. Cambridge: Cambridge University Press, 2006.

———. *Galilee and Gospel: Collected Essays*. Heidelberg: Mohr Siebeck, 2000.

———. *Jesus, A Jewish Galilean: A New Reading of the Jesus Story*. Edinburgh: T&T Clark, 2004.

Froissart, Jean. *Chronicles of England, France, Spain, and the Adjoining Countries*. Translated by Thomas Johnes. London: Longman, Hurst, Rees, and Orme, 1805.

Garland, David E. *Exegetical Commentary on the New Testament: Luke*. Zondervan Exegetical Commentary on the New Testament series. Grand Rapids: Zondervan, 2011.

Glatzer, Nahum, editor. *The Passover Haggadah. With English Translation and Commentary. Based on the Commentaries of E.D. Goldschmidt*. 3d ed. New York: Schocken, 1979.

Graeber, David. *Debt: the first 5000 years*. Brooklyn: Melville House, 2015.

———. *TheUtopia of Rules: On Technology, Stupidity, and the Secret Joys of Bureaucracy*. Brooklyn: Melville House, 2016.

———. *Toward and Anthropological Theory of Value: The False Coin of our own Dreams*. New York: Palgrave, 2001.

Gudeman, Stephen. *The Anthropology of the Economy*. Hoboken: Wiley-Blackwell, 2001.

Hann, Chris and Hart, Keith. *Economic Anthropology*. Cambridge: Polity, 2011.

Herodotus. *Histories*. Translated by Rawlinson. London: Penguin Classics, 2003.

Herzog II, William R. "Why Peasants Responded to Jesus." In *A People's History of Christianity: Christian Origins*, edited by Richard Horsley. Minneapolis: Fortress, 2005.

Holmes W., Michael. "Polycarp's Letter to the Philippians and the Writings that later formed the New Testament." In *The Reception of the New Testament in the Apostolic Fathers*, edited by Andrew F. Gregory and Christopher M. Tuckett. Oxford: Oxford University Press, 2005.

Horsley, Richard. "Jesus Movements and the Renewal of Israel." In *A People's History of Christianity: Christian Origins*, edited by Richard Horsley. Minneapolis: Fortress, 2005.

———. *Jesus and the Spiral of Violence: Popular Resistance in Roman Palestine*. Minneapolis: Fortress, 1993.

Isocrates. "Nicocles or the Cyprians." Translated by George Norlin. In *Isocrates, Volume I: To Demonicus. To Nicocles. Nicocles or the Cyprians. Panegyricus. To Philip. Archidamus*. Loeb Classical Library. Cambridge: Harvard University Press, 1928.

Jensen, Morten. *Herod Antipas in Galilee*. Heidelberg: Mohr Siebeck, 2006.

Josephus. "Antiquities." In *The Works of Josephus, Complete and Unabridged New Updated Edition*. Translated by William Whiston. Peabody: Hendrickson, 1987.

———. "War of the Jews." In *The Works of Josephus, Complete and Unabridged New Updated Edition*. Translated by William Whiston. Peabody: Hendrickson, 1987.

Justin Martyr. "First Apology." Translated by Marcus Dods and George Reith. In *Ante-Nicene Christian Library Vol. 1*, edited by Alexander Roberts, James Donaldson, and A. Cleveland Coxe. Buffalo: Christian Literature Publishing Company, 1885.

Kalinowski, Angela. "Patterns of Patronage The Politics and Ideology of Public Building in the Eastern Roman Empire (31 BCE – 600 CE)." Phd Diss., University of Toronto, 1996.

Kloppenborg John. *The formation of Q: Trajectories in Ancient Wisdom Collections*. Minneapolis: Fortress, 1987.

———. *Q the Earliest Gospel : An Introduction to the Original Stories and Sayings of Jesus*. Louisville: Westminster John Knox, 2008.

Leslie J., Hoppe. *There Shall Be No Poor Among You: Poverty in the Bible.* Nashville: Abingdon Press, 2004.

Levine, Amy Jill. "Introduction." In *The Historical Jesus in Context,* edited by Amy Jill Levine, Dale C. Allison, John Dominic Crossan. Princeton: Princeton University Press, 2009.

Levi-Strauss, Claude. *The Elementary structures of Kinship.* London: Eyre & Spottiswodde, 1969.

Long A.A. and Sedley D.N. *The Hellenistic Philosophies: Volume 1 Translations of the Principal Sources with Philosophical Commentary.* Cambridge: Cambridge University Press, 1987.

Lucian. "*The Passing of Peregrinus.*" In *Lucian Vol. 5.* Translated by A.M. Hamron. New York: Putnam's, London: Heinemann, 1925.

Mack, Burton. *The Lost Gospel: The Book of Q and Christian Origins.* New York: Harpercollins. 1993.

Malina, Bruce J. *The New Testament World: Insights from Cultural Anthropology.* Louisville: Westminster John Knox, 2001.

———. *The Social World of Jesus and the Gospels.* Abingdon: Routledge, 1996.

Marshall, Howard I. *The Gospel of Luke: A Commentary on the Greek Text.* The New International Greek Commentary. Grand Rapids: Eerdmans, 1978.

Mauss, Marcel. *The Gift: The Form and Reason for Exchange in Archaic Societies.* Abingdon: Routledge, 2002.

May, Simon. *Love: A History.* New Haven: Yale University Press, 2013.

McCollough, Thomas C. "City and Village in Lower Galilee: The Import of the Archeological Excavations at Sepphoris and Khirbet Qana (Cana) for Framing the Economic Context of Jesus." In *The Galilean Economy in the time of Jesus,* edited by David A. Fiensy and Ralph K. Hawkins. Atlanta: SBL Press, 2013.

Meier, John P. *A Marginal Jew: Rethinking the Historical Jesus, Volume 1: The Roots of the Problem and the Person.* The Anchor Yale Bible Reference Library. New Haven: Yale University Press, 1991.

Meyes, Eric and Chancey, Mark. *Alexander to Constantine: Archaeology of the Land of the Bible.* New Haven: Yale University Press, 2009.

Montero, Roman. *All Things in Common: The Economic Practices of the Early Christians.* Eugene: Resource Publications, 2017.

Morley, Neville. "The Poor in the city of Rome." In *Poverty in the Roman World,* edited by Atkins, Margaret and Osborne, Robin. Cambridge: Cambridge University Press, 2006.

Neusner, Jacob. *Judaism: The Evidence of the Mishnah.* Eugene: Wipf & Stock, 2003.

Oakman, Douglas E. *Jesus and the Peasants.* Matrix: The Bible in Mediterranean Context 4. Eugene: Cascade Books, 2008.

O'keefe, Tim. *Epicureanism.* Ancient Philosophies. Berkeley: University of California Press, 2009.

Origen. "Against Celsus." Translated by Frederik Crombie. In *Ante-Nicene Christian Library Vol. 4,* edited by Alexander Roberts, James Donaldson, and A. Cleveland Coxe. Buffalo: Christian Literature Publishing Company, 1885.

Parkin, Anneliese. "You do him no Service." In *Poverty in the Roman World,* edited by Atkins, Margaret and Osborne, Robin. Cambridge: Cambridge University Press, 2006.

Patterson, Thomas C. "Distribution and Redistribution." In *A Handbook of Economic Anthropology,* edited by James G. Carrier. Cheltenham: Edward Elgar, 2014.

Pelagius. "On Riches." In *Pelagius: Life and Letters.* Translated by B.R. Rees. Suffolk: Boydell & Brewer Press, 2004.

Philo. "On Virtues." In *The Works of Philo Judaeus: The Contemporary of Josephus, Translated from the Greek.* Translated by Charles Duke Yonge. London: George Bell and Sons, 1890.

Plato. "Gorgias." Translated by Donald J. Zeyl. In *Plato: Complete Works,* edited by John M. Cooper and D.S. Hutchinson. Cambridge: Hackett Publishing Company, 1997.

———. "Laws." Translated by Trevor J. Schofield. In *Plato: Complete Works,* edited by John M. Cooper and D.S. Hutchinson. Cambridge: Hackett Publishing Company, 1997.

——— "Republic." Translated by G.M.A Grube and C.D.C. Reeve. In *Plato: Complete Works,* edited by John M. Cooper and D.S. Hutchinson. Cambridge: Hackett Publishing Company, 1997.

Pseudo Johnathan. "Jerusalem Targum on Leviticus." In *The Targums of Onkelos and Jonathan ben Uzziel on the Pentateuch: with the fragments of the Jerusalem Targum from the Chaldee.* Translated by J.W. Etheridge. London: Longman, Green, Longman, Roberts, and Green, 1862.

Reed, Johnathan L. "Archaeological Contributions to the Study of Jesus and the Gospels." In *The Historical Jesus in Context,* edited by Amy Jill Levine, Dale C. Allison, John Dominic Crossan. Princeton: Princeton University Press, 2009.

Robinson James M. "Kerygma and History in the New Testament." In *Trajectories through Early Christianity,* edited by James M. Robinson and Helmut Koester. Eugene: Wipf & Stock, 2006.

Root, Bradley W. *First-Century Galilee: A Fresh Examination of the Sources.* Wissenschaftliche Untersuchungen Zum Neuen Testament 2.Reihe. Heidelberg: Mohr Siebeck, 2014.

Sanders, E.P. *Jewish Law from Jesus to the Mishnah: Five Studies.* London: SCM Press, 1990.

Seneca. "Moral Epistles to Lucilius." In *Epistulae Morales: Letters LXVI-XCII vol. 2.* Translated by Richard. M Gummere. Cambridge: Harvard University Press, 1920.

———. "On Benefits Book II." In *L. Annaeus Seneca On Benefits.* Translated by Aubrey Stewart, M.A. London: George Bell and Sons, 1887.

——— "On Clemency 1." In *L. Annaeus Seneca, Minor Dialogs Together with the Dialog "On Clemency."* Translated by Aubrey Stewart. London: George Bell and Sons, 1990.

———. "On Clemency 2." In *L. Annaeus Seneca, Minor Dialogs Together with the Dialog "On Clemency."* Translated by Aubrey Stewart. London: George Bell and Sons, 1990.

Shawn J. Wilhite. "Didache." in *The Lexham Bible Dictionary,* edited by John D Barry. Bellingham: Lexham Press, 2016.

Simmons, William. "Taxation." in *The Lexham Bible Dictionary,* edited by John D Barry. Bellingham: Lexham Press, 2016.

Stark, Rodney. *The Triumph of Christianity: How the Jesus Movement Became the World's Largest Religion.* New York: Harpercollins, 2011.

Stobaeus. *Ioannis Stobaei Anthology, Vol 3,* edited by Curtius Wachsmuth and Otto Hense. Berlin: Weidmannsche Buchhandlung, 1912.

Swift, Louis J. *The Early Fathers on War and Military Service.* Message of the Fathers of the Church. Wilmington: Michael Glazier, 1983.

Tacitus. "Annals." In *The Modern Library: Complete works of Tacitus*. Translated by Alfred John Church and William Jackson Brodribb. New York: Random House, 1942.

Talbert, Charles H. *Reading Luke: A Literary and Theological Commentary on the Third Gospel*. Reading the New Testament. Macon: Smtyh & Helwys, 2013.

Tertullian. "Apology." Translated by S. Thelwall. In *Ante-Nicene Christian Library Vol. 3*, edited by Alexander Roberts, James Donaldson, and A. Cleveland Coxe. Buffalo: Christian Literature Publishing Company, 1885.

———. "De Corona." Translated by S. Thelwall. In *Ante-Nicene Christian Library Vol. 3*, edited by Alexander Roberts, James Donaldson, and A. Cleveland Coxe. Buffalo: Christian Literature Publishing Company, 1885.

———. "On Idolatry." Translated by S. Thelwall. In *Ante-Nicene Christian Library Vol. 3*, edited by Alexander Roberts, James Donaldson, and A. Cleveland Coxe. Buffalo: Christian Literature Publishing Company, 1885.

Tuckett, Christopher M. *Q and the History of Early Christianity*. Peabody: Hendrickson, 1996.

Whitehead, Neil L. "the Poetics of Violence." In *Violence*, edited by Whitehead, Neil L. Santa Fe: School of American Research, 2004.

Witherington III, Ben. *New Testament History: A Narrative Account*. Grand Rapids: Baker Academic, 2003.

Woolf, Greg. "Writing Poverty in Rome." In *Poverty in the Roman World*, edited by Atkins, Margaret and Osborne, Robin. Cambridge: Cambridge University Press, 2006.

Xenophon. "Oeconomicus II." In *Xenophon: Memorabilia, Oeconomicus, Symposium, Apologia*. Translated by F.C. Merchant and O.J. Todd. Cambridge: Harvard University Press, 1923.

Yoder, John Howard. *The politics of Jesus*. Grand Rapids: Eerdmans, 2004.

Index of Ancient Documents

-

Made in United States
North Haven, CT
24 January 2023

31582771R00095